Challenging puzzles

Colin Vout and Gordon Gray

CAMBRIDGE
UNIVERSITY PRESS

Published by the Press Syndicate of the University of Cambridge
The Pitt Building, Trumpington Street, Cambridge CB2 1RP
40 West 20th Street, New York, NY 10011-4211, USA
10 Stamford Road, Oakleigh, Melbourne 3166, Australia

First published 1993

Printed in Great Britain by Scotprint Ltd, Musselburgh, Scotland

A catalogue record for this book is available from the British Library

Library of Congress cataloguing in publication data

Vout, Colin, 1953–
Challenging puzzles / Colin Vout and Gordon Gray.
    p.   cm.
ISBN 0 521 44602 3
1. Mathematical recreations. 2. Puzzles. I. Gray, Gordon, 1952– II. Title.
QA95.V68 1993
793.7′4 - dc20 92 - 46565 CIP

ISBN 0 521 44602 3

Cover illustration by Simon Larkin

Text cartoons by Harry Venning

VN

Contents

Introduction

The puzzles in this book are based on a series that a group of us at work set for each other to solve. A problem was set every Friday lunchtime as a challenge for those present to solve, and the winner was obliged to set the puzzle the following week. Half of the puzzles here come from that source, and half have been composed especially for the book. All of the problems are believed to be original, and, except for the game 'dodgem', none have been published before.

The levels of the problems vary considerably. There are new versions of old ideas, and new ideas and diversions. For some questions you need to work methodically along well-defined lines, and for others you need flashes of inspiration to make progress. Some can be done in five minutes, and others suggest areas that could keep you entertained for five weeks. Different types of problems appear – many are mathematical but others involve logic, words, games and pattern-making.

Easy and hard problems are interspersed throughout the book, but a list is included that gives each problem a grading according to the rough degree of difficulty. These gradings are subjective and perhaps rather approximate; in some problems where you have to score as highly as possible, and in all of the games, it is quite easy to find one solution, but quite tricky to find the best.

The subject-matter of the problems may be just numbers, or letters, or both. In one chapter you are taken into the world of the seven dwarfs, who happen to bear some resemblance to the writers of the book. In another you will learn the fascinations of the isle of Maranga, which is claimed to be the only island in puzzledom not inhabited by liars and truth-tellers. Among the rest there are problems on sports, games and the sex life of Martians.

Finally, if you enjoy solving these puzzles half as much as we've enjoyed setting them, and we've enjoyed solving each other's three-quarters as much as we've enjoyed setting them, and the measure of how much we've enjoyed solving each other's is a whole number whose digits . . . Oh, never mind! Good luck!

Credits

The main puzzle setters were, in alphabetical order:

Barry Clarke   (the puzzle that started it all, no. 1)

Gordon Gray   (seven dwarfs concept and basic plot, and nos. 13, 14, 22 (half), 23, 24, 25, 29, 33 (half), 34, 37, 40, 45, 46, 48, 51, 57, 68, 74, 76, 78, 81, 85, 89 and 91)

Keith Lipscombe (nos. 7, 27 and 32)

Neil Otway   (the island puzzle that led to no. 54, and nos. 5, 8, 77, 80, 83, 87 and 94)

Ian Parsons   (nos. 10, 30 and 72)

Colin Vout   (overall editing, seven dwarfs plot integration, Maranga concept, Martian concept, Hints and Coda chapters, and nos. 2, 9, 11, 16, 17, 18, 19, 20, 22 (half), 26, 28, 31, 33 (half), 35, 36, 38, 39, 41, 42, 43, 44, 47, 49, 50, 52, 53, 54, 55, 56, 58, 59, 60, 61, 62, 63, 64, 65, 66, 67, 69, 70, 71, 73, 75, 79, 82, 84, 86, 90, 92, 93, 95, 96, 97, 99 and 100)

Martin Wallace   (nos. 3, 4, 6, 12, 15, 21 and 88)

In addition, Nic Towers contributed no. 98, and Christopher Hills helped to fine-tune the game 'dodgem', many years ago.

The problems have been road-tested by the main setters, and the help of Alison Lister, Theo Gray, Sonia Hartman and Julian Bright is also gratefully acknowledged.

The authors and publishers are grateful to Samuel French Ltd for permission to include the quotation on page 113.

Guide to the puzzles

You may choose to do the puzzles in order, following the narratives and linking themes through the chapters. Or, like someone with a box of chocolates, you may prefer to start with the ones that have wrappings or decorations that appeal to you most, and go back and finish the rest afterwards. If, however, you have a particular preference for soft centres or hard centres, then the following list may help. The problems are graded from one star up to five star, with the titles listed and grouped by the chapter in which they occur.

For each of the puzzles, there is help available in the hints chapter. The hints assist to different extents for different problems, but the star grading for a puzzle refers to the problem *without* the hint. Even if you have found the solution, you can consult the hint, which occasionally gives parts of the answer; if you are wrong, this will let you reattempt the problem without having been told the whole solution.

In a few cases, the problem doesn't end at the solution. Seven of the problems are taken a stage further, in a chapter that follows the chapter of solutions. There, you will find some generalizations, discussions and questions for your own investigation.

ONE-STAR PUZZLES

These are the puzzles to get you off to a gentle start. They almost constitute a maths-free zone!

	Chapter 1		
2	Colour change	16	Three by three
3	Missing number I	18	Words myths
5	Missing letter I		
6	Coining a word		*Chapter 2*
8	Hasty words	19	Mirror on the wall
9	Missing letter II	20	Lost in the woods
11	War of words	21	The dwarfs' heights
13	Palindromic equation	24	The wrong rooms
15	Building structures	34	To the dungeons
		35	Freeing Snow White

TWO-STAR PUZZLES

A little more effort is needed for these, but the route to the solution should be straightforward to find. A fun run for the brain!

THREE-STAR PUZZLES

You are now entering an area where the solutions are more closely guarded. Be prepared to be challenged at any time!

FOUR-STAR PUZZLES

Some ingenuity and application is needed for these. Arm yourself with a few spare sheets of paper before attempting them!

FIVE-STAR PUZZLES

These certainly need inspiration and perspiration, but never desperation. Be prepared to come back to them on a second day!

1 Starters

1 Missing digit
What is the missing digit in this sequence?

5, 8, 3, −, 2, 1

2 Colour change
Turn from BLACK to WHITE in the minimum number of moves, changing one letter at each step and leaving a genuine English word at each stage.

3 Missing number I
What is the missing number in this series?

0, 1, 4, 15, −, 325

4 Coded quote
Decode the following to find an apt quotation.

17,11   20,9   5,1,2   10,9,1,23,23,24
16,2,7,9,10,12,14,1,2,7   14,15,9   6,10,4,3,23,9,25 , 14,15,9
1,2,12,20,9,10   20,17,23,23   5,4,25,9   4,16,14   4,11
17,14 , 3,9,5,1,16,12,9   14,15,9   1,2,12,20,9,10   17,12
2,4,14   12,9,6,1,10,1,14,9   11,10,4,25   14,15,9
8,16,9,12,14,17,4,2

5   Missing letter I

Fill in the gap in this sequence of letters:

M, V, –, M, J, S, U, N, P

6   Coining a word

Get from HEAD to TAIL in as few goes as possible (rules as in puzzle no. 2).

7   Missing number II

What is the missing number?

90, 96, 43, 56, 39, 50, 68, 89, –, 78, 94, 55

8   Hasty words

In fifteen minutes, form as many words as you can from the letters of CHALLENGING PUZZLES. All words must have more than three letters. Participles and plurals are not allowed (so that prohibits CHALLENGING and PUZZLES!). How well you do will be judged by the total number of letters in all of your words.

9   Missing letter II

What is the next letter in this sequence?

O, I, Z, E, H, S, G, –

10   Missing number III

What is the next number in this series?

75, 73, 69, 72, 67, 68, 70, –

11 War of words

Change from the Roman god of war, MARS, into the Greek one, ARES, in as few turns as possible (rules as for puzzle no. 2).

12 Missing letters

Fill in the gaps in the following sequence:

A, E, A, –, A, U, U, U, E, –, O, E

13 Palindromic equation

If $ab + cd = efg$ and $gf + ed = cba$, where each letter represents a digit (not necessarily all different), then what are the values of the letters?

14 Missing letter III

What is the missing letter?

A, F, H, I, K, –, Y, Z

15   Building structures

Change BRICK into STONE in as few moves as possible (rules as for puzzle no. 2).

16   Three by three

Find three three-digit square numbers that together use each of the digits 1, 2, 3, . . . , 9 exactly once.

17   Missing numbers

What are the next two numbers in this sequence?
1, 4, 3, 11, 15, 13, 17, 24, 23, –, –

18   Words myths

Go from the Greek goddess, HERA, to her Roman equivalent, JUNO, in the minimum number of moves (rules as for puzzle no. 2).

2 The adventures of the seven dwarfs

19 Mirror on the wall

The queen sat before her magic mirror, as she had on many occasions before, ready to ask it her favourite question. She had had a hard day ordering her subjects around, but it gave her a great sense of a job well done to see the resentment and annoyance she caused. The only person who was rather unsatisfying to order about was her stepdaughter, Snow White. Snow White was always helpful, pleasant and obedient, and she grew more beautiful every day.

The queen addressed the mirror: 'Who is the fairest in all the land?' Six letters formed along the bottom of the mirror, each changing in sequence through the alphabet, A to B to C to . . . to Y to Z to A and so on. Eventually they stopped, in the usual pattern, Q–U–E–E–N– followed by the queen's initial. Her smile of satisfaction rapidly turned to a frown of worry, though, as the letters started moving again, each changing by a certain amount, the amounts seeming to be in a logical progression. The frown turned to a stare of horror when she read the letters that had now appeared: S–W–H–I–T–E.

There and then, the queen decided she would do away with her stepdaughter. But what was the queen's initial?

20 Lost in the woods

Snow White shivered as she followed the palace servant on what she believed was a simple walk through the woods. The queen had ordered him to murder Snow White, but he couldn't bring himself to get the deed over with. He regretted the awful marriage the king had made after Snow White's mother had died, and a deep love remained for the former queen in the hearts of many of those at court. Finally he said to himself, 'No matter what the queen may compel, I cannot murder Snow White; but how will the queen know whether I do? Doubtless I could lie to her when I return.' He hesitated for a second or two, then told Snow White the truth, rushed away, and left her on her own.

Snow White was lost in the woods, alone, and didn't feel at all brave, not knowing what her next move should be. It was already a bitter night, and then the rain began. Nettles abounded, and they would make poor substitutes for her former linen sheets that night; the berries and nuts would provide a dismal larder. Snow White looked around, and found a tree very good for sheltering under, as the rain was falling faster now, leaving her wet and cold. Was God with her? She would soon find out.

The only comfort for Snow White was the birds she spotted in the woods. Can you find twenty birds hidden in consecutive letters of the previous two paragraphs?

21   The dwarfs' heights

Deep in the woods, and not far from where Snow White rested that night, was the cottage of the seven dwarfs. Their names were Bossy, Doc, Dopey, Dozey, Grumpy, Hairy and Jock. They spent that evening in their usual ways, never expecting that the next day a visitor might come and change the routine in their little house.

The house was so little because the dwarfs were really very small themselves. For instance, Jock was 1 foot 10 inches, Dopey was 2 feet 4 inches, Hairy was 2 feet 8 inches and Bossy was 1 foot 2 inches tall. How tall were Dozey, Grumpy and Doc?

22   Snow White arrives

It was late the next morning before Snow White stumbled on the dwarfs' cottage. The seven dwarfs were all fast asleep, having worn themselves out by drinking too much tea. They were awakened by a knocking at their front door, and, when they opened it, they saw a beautiful young girl.

'Hello, my name's Snow White,' she announced, 'and I must hide from my stepmother, the evil queen, who wants to kill me. I expect you've heard about me.'

The dwarfs hadn't, but were far too polite to say so. 'Do come in, and tell us what we can do for you,' said Bossy.

Snow White explained that she was looking for somewhere to stay, and had seen their delightful little cottage. Naturally the dwarfs felt bound to invite her to stay with them; they had a guest room that would be just right for her. But there were mixed feelings among the dwarfs, because some of them were worried that they would miss their lunchtime exercise that day. The dwarfs had simple tastes and they really looked forward to their lunchtime game of cards. However, everyone was pleased when Snow White agreed to join them in their modest little game.

Starting with a normal pack of cards, the two and three of clubs and the two and three of diamonds were removed, and then six cards were dealt to each person. Each player looked at his (or her) cards and passed on three of them to the player on his (or her) left. No player was allowed to pass on the queen of spades (who looked disturbingly like the evil queen herself).

After the passing of cards, no-one held a singleton card, or indeed all six cards in the same suit. Four people held spades, and one suit was held only by Dopey, Hairy and Doc. Bossy held fewer court cards than Snow White, but there was no suit in which he held a lower court card than Snow White did. Dozey had identical cards in three suits. Jock had every one of his cards paired with the other of the same colour. Grumpy was not pleased to have the top three clubs.

When the players had assessed their cards, a game based upon whist was played. Snow White found she quite enjoyed it. The question is, though, who had the queen of spades?

23   The dwarfs' rooms

After the game of cards, the dwarfs showed Snow White the sleeping quarters, or eighths as they actually were. There was one central room, the guest room, and arranged regularly around it were seven little rooms, one for each dwarf. From the central room, Snow White could see the names on the doors, in alphabetical order – Bossy, Doc, Dopey, Dozey, Grumpy, Hairy and Jock – as shown in the diagram.

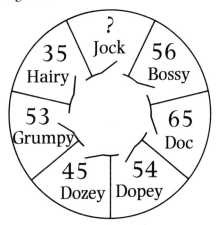

'That will do splendidly for me, thank you very much,' said Snow White. Then she added, 'You know, I think you should have numbers on the doors as well.'

The dwarfs thought that going from 1 to 7 was a little too ordinary, so they all went to their rooms to think about it. After lengthy consideration, each of them came up with a number, and each with the same logical reason. The diagram shows the numbers for most of the dwarfs, but what was Jock's number?

24   The wrong rooms

At the end of the day, Snow White and the seven dwarfs all went to their rooms as planned, with Snow White in the central room and the dwarfs in alphabetical order around her. But there were mischievous thoughts in the air.

Just before midnight, one of the doors creaked open, and Bossy crept into Snow White's room. To his horror, another of the doors opened, so he hid under the bed. Then another door opened, and another, until all the dwarfs except one were hiding under the bed, and Doc alone was left standing. As Doc moved towards the bed, he tripped, stirring Snow White from her slumbers. The dwarfs panicked, and all attempted to flee from the room.

However, in their confusion, they all went to different, but wrong, doorways. Indeed, all of them missed their own room by more than one door. Grumpy and Dopey both finished opposite their own rooms and next to each other, while Bossy and Doc also finished opposite their own rooms but not next to each other.

Snow White had been disturbed but not woken; she slept soundly through the night, while the dwarfs stayed where they were, alone. Who spent the night in Grumpy's room?

25   Who led that?

At lunchtime the next day, some of the dwarfs were showing Snow White round the woods, and only four of them stayed behind to play cards: just Jock, Doc, Grumpy and Bossy. Several hands had been played and a card, the seven of diamonds, lay on the table.

'Who led that?' asked Grumpy.

Bossy muttered something.

Doc said, 'Bossy led it.'

Jock said that Bossy had told him that Grumpy had led it.

'No, it wasn't me, or Jock,' said Grumpy.

'As I said before, it was Doc,' said Bossy.

In fact, only one of the dwarfs had been speaking truthfully. So who had led the seven of diamonds?

PROTECTING SNOW WHITE

26   Sick leave

That evening, the dwarfs had a big discussion. They realized that Snow White would need protection, but the next day was Monday and they were all expected back at work in the chocolate mines. Worse than that, the hot season was starting, and they were needed to work seven days a week for some time to get the chocolate out – there had been a lot of popular concern about the possibility of a melt-down, and the devastation that a chocolate fall-out could cause.

In the end they decided there was nothing else for it. At all times, two of the dwarfs would have to stay behind to guard Snow White during the coming fortnight. They would do this by each dwarf sending in a message that he was sick – they could say that there was a bug going round the cottage – at some time during the period. Each dwarf would stay off work for a different length of time, from one to seven days. To ensure that there were always two off work on any day, whenever one dwarf returned to work, another would start taking leave.

So, Hairy and Grumpy sent in messages saying they were sick on the first Monday. Doc started his leave on the Tuesday, Jock on the Friday, and Bossy on the Sunday. Dozey said he was sick after that, and Dopey two days after him. On which day did Dopey start his leave?

27   The melted bar

One day during the hot weather the dwarfs decided they'd like a special treat to eat, and Hairy remembered that he had stored a rectangular slab of chocolate in the chocolate cupboard some time before. A lively debate began on how to divide up the slab between them, given that it was twice as wide as it was high, and twice as long as it was wide.

Hairy and Dopey went to fetch the chocolate. As they opened the cupboard, the clock struck an hour, as Hairy remembered it had done when he had put the slab inside. But it was apparent that tragedy also had struck. While the slab had been in the cupboard, it had melted in the hot weather into a new shape. It was still cuboid and the new length was similarly twice the new width, but the height – ughh! Doc pointed out that a slab had once been left in the cupboard in similar weather for five whole days, and the height had steadily dwindled away to nothing. The volume had remained the same throughout, though, he remarked cheerily.

The dwarfs decided to divide the whole slab into an exact number of chunks, by making a number of equally spaced slices along the length and width. Each chunk would be the height of the melted slab, and have a square cross-section with its side being four times the height. How many chunks were there, and how long had the slab been in the cupboard?

28   The old lady and the apples

After the fortnight of guarding Snow White closely, the dwarfs considered that the danger had passed, and that it was safe to leave her alone while they went out to work. The chocolate mining over for now, their main work was prospecting, which often meant irregular hours.

One afternoon Snow White was alone in the cottage when there was a knock on the door. She answered it, and saw a little old lady with a basket of apples. The lady's head was covered with a shawl, but the face seemed vaguely familiar, although maybe this was just because it looked a bit like a picture she had seen on a pack of cards.

'Would you like one of my apples, my dear?' enquired the old lady, offering the one right in the middle of the basket. The apples were arranged very regularly, with six apples in a ring round the middle one, and another twelve in a ring round those, as you can see in the diagram.

'I hope they haven't been grown with the aid of fertilizers that pollute the environment,' said Snow White, who was concerned about things like that.

'Oh, definitely not. There are no chemicals, except that some of them have been coated with something to kill pests,' replied the old lady, with a grin.

'Well, that apple looks very nice,' said Snow White, reaching out her hand to take one; but just as she was about to touch it, the old lady rotated the basket so that a different one was selected instead. Snow White dithered, and decided on another one, but the old lady rotated the basket again, and so the process repeated for some time. The whole thing went like this:

Snow White	Little old lady
chose an apple	rotated basket a sixth of a turn clockwise
chose the next anticlockwise in the same ring	rotated basket a sixth of a turn clockwise
chose one three apples away	rotated half a turn
chose the next clockwise	rotated a sixth of a turn anticlockwise
chose one three apples away	rotated half a turn
chose one three apples away	did nothing
chose the next anticlockwise	

'My, you're quite an indecisive young girl, aren't you?' said the old lady, with perhaps just a hint of exasperation in her voice. 'Why don't we start all over again, and you try to make up your mind a little bit faster this time?' She presented the basket again to Snow White, but another episode followed.

Snow White	Little old lady
chose an apple	rotated basket a sixth of a turn clockwise
chose the next anticlockwise	rotated basket a sixth of a turn clockwise
chose the next anticlockwise	did nothing
chose an apple next to the last two	rotated basket a sixth of a turn anticlockwise
chose the next anticlockwise	rotated basket a third of a turn anticlockwise
chose the next anticlockwise	did nothing

chose the apple symmetrically opposite	rotated basket a sixth of a turn clockwise
picked up the apple	did nothing

Just then there was an unexpected call: 'Hallo, Snow White, I'm home early today! And who's this with you? Someone handing out free apples, I'll be bound.' It was Hairy, who in fact had seen the whole exchange, and had realized what was going on: Snow White was picking the apples more or less at random, but the old lady was trying to force a choice on her, so that she took one of a certain set of the apples. Obviously some of the apples were not very good ones for Snow White! If Snow White's choice pleased the old lady, she did nothing; but if it displeased her, she moved the basket to make Snow White go for an apple that did please her.

'Put back that apple, I'll choose one for you, and one for each of us dwarfs too,' said Hairy, and Snow White replaced the apple she had taken in the left half of the second row from her. Hairy then selected eight apples and bade good-day to the disgruntled old lady. Which eight apples?

29 The Dark Tower

The dwarfs had been badly shaken by Snow White's narrow escape. They decided that various preparations should be made, one being to assess the possibility of using the Dark Tower as a look-out post. This imposing structure stood on an open flat plain, and had ivy growing round its upper reaches like a shaggy beard, giving it the appearance of great antiquity. In fact, it stood above one of the disused chocolate mines, whose rich veins had long since yielded up all their valuable supply.

'What exactly are we meant to be doing here?' grumbled Grumpy to Doc.

'Hairy reckons that we need to measure its height,' came the reply.

Doc had taken Dopey, Grumpy and Dozey with him on the expedition. 'Well, I'm certainly not going to climb up it,' said Dozey. Doc stood puzzled for a while as the other three moved apart and gazed up at the top of the tower.

'If it's any help, I can judge from the angle to the top that my distance from the base is five times its height,' volunteered Dopey.

'For that matter, my distance from the base is two and a half times the height,' added Dozey.

'I was just going to say that too!' grumbled Grumpy.

Doc suddenly brightened up. Looking at the positions of the other dwarfs, he could see that each of the three of them was exactly 100 yards from the other two. So what was the height of the Dark Tower, to the nearest foot?

30   Foiling the traps

To make sure that Snow White was safe, the dwarfs realized that they could no longer leave her alone in the house. So whenever they all had to go out, they made certain that she came with them. This frequently meant leaving the cottage unattended, and no-one noticed a certain character creeping in on seven consecutive days, staying for a little while, and then leaving.

When the time came for the weekly cleaning of the cottage, Grumpy felt hard done by because it was his turn. 'For all the other weeks, Snow White has been doing a little light dusting each day, and that's made your job a lot easier,' he grumbled. 'This week I've got a lot to do, all by myself.'

'Tell you what,' said Dozey. 'Let's all have a nice cup of tea, and then at six o'clock we'll all join in, and give everything a really thorough cleaning.'

That is what they did, and it was just as well. One by one, each dwarf discovered a booby trap designed to finish off poor Snow White. One such trap had been laid each day the certain character had entered the cottage.

The trap laid on Saturday was an arrangement of magnifying glass and some straw in Snow White's room, so that on the day the Sun was high enough, its early morning rays would be focused to start a fire.

It hadn't been on the Tuesday that the bridge over the stream had been sawn almost through.

The cunning arrangement of spikes in Snow White's bedsprings, intended to uncoil at some future date, was the third trap to have been set.

Grumpy discovered the trap that had been set second.

The trap that Dozey discovered had not been set on a day beginning with a T or an S.

The trap set on Friday was discovered nine minutes before the explosives in the fire were.

The sixth trap had been set on Monday.

Dopey found a trap sixteen minutes after Dozey did.

Jock discovered the scorpion in Snow White's dressing table, and it had been put there on Monday.

The trap laid on Wednesday was discovered at twenty-one minutes past six, but not by Bossy or Doc.

Hairy discovered a trap four minutes after Doc did, and eleven minutes after Tuesday's trap was uncovered.

The first trap to have been set was the explosives in the fire, but it wasn't found by Dozey.

Dopey found the trap set on Sunday, two minutes after Jock found his.

The noose and tripwire in the woods was found two minutes before the heavy weight balanced on the wardrobe door.

Who found what, when, and when had it been set?

BATTLE IS JOINED

31   The queen attacks!

'To hell with subtlety!' stormed the queen. 'All of my clever plans have failed, so let's try something a bit more direct!' Her strategy was probably correct, because to get what you want you often have to use a bit of subtlety and then some brute force. 'I must finish off that Snow White creature, so, generals, assemble your troops!'

She was addressing the seven generals of the realm, and planning a massive strike against the dwarfs' cottage. Outside the palace, each general joined his section of troops, and with the generals included they were able to form into seven identical squares. Then the queen swept down the palace steps and joined the army; with her included, they were able to rearrange themselves into a single large square.

And so off to battle marched the huge army, at least ten thousand strong, although not as many as a hundred thousand. Surely nothing could save Snow White and her seven dwarf friends? Unless, of course, they knew the exact number of people marching against them. Which was . . .?

32   The dwarfs defend!

The dwarfs held a council of war when they learnt of the attack. By now the advancing army had separated again into its seven squares, and the queen was nowhere to be seen. Obviously the dwarfs had some square-bashing to do if they were to survive.

'How can we rout the squares?' asked Bossy.

'Divide them by a number that gives itself as a result,' said Doc, half in jest.

The dwarfs agreed that this was a desperate plan, but the only chance they had. Force was out of the question, so a little magic would be needed. To give themselves heart, they chanted out their names together:

DOPEY, DOZEY, GRUMPY, JOCK,
BOSSY, HAIRY, then comes DOC!

Each dwarf would take on one of the generals, and would use the letters of his own name to form the number of men on the side of the general's square (that is, the side of the seven identical squares into which the army had formed).

After some thought, each dwarf rearranged the letters of his name as appropriate, translated them to numbers by $A = 1$, $B = 2$, . . ., $Z = 26$, and employed addition, subtraction, multiplication, division and bracketing as necessary, to form the all-important number. (One of Dopey's first attempts was $P \times E - (O + Y)/D = 16 \times 5 - (15 + 25)/4 = 70$, but since 70 wasn't the required number, this didn't work.)

Can you find a formula for each dwarf's name that would give the correct number?

33   Captured generals

Amazingly, the dwarfs' plan succeeded! No sooner had they chalked suitable formulae inside mystic heptagrams, than all the soldiers, apart from the generals themselves, mysteriously disappeared. Each dwarf then rushed at his general, brandishing his pick from the chocolate mine, and made short work of him. Their resistance over, the generals were marched to the dwarfs' cottage.

The dwarfs decided that a seminar on the nature of good and evil would be very beneficial for the generals, and also a suitable punishment. It was arranged that each dwarf would give a short lecture on one topic, with, of course, appropriate breaks for tea and biscuits.

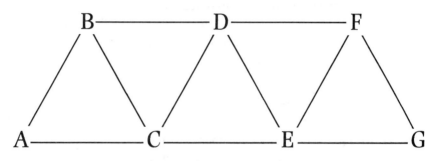

They sat the seven generals – who were named Archibald, Benedict, Cornelius, Dominic, Ethelbert, Farquhar and Gervase – in positions as shown in the diagram, for the first lecture. However, there was a worry that any three of the generals might together have enough brain cells to hatch a plot, and that it would therefore be dangerous for any trio of generals to occur in a triangle more than once during the seminar.

So, can you find arrangements of the generals for the second, third, . . ., seventh lectures, so that no three generals ever appear together in a triangle more than once?

34   To the dungeons

'A marvellous performance, fellow-dwarfs,' exclaimed Bossy, as he made everyone double-strength tea to celebrate.

'I knew my research into thaumaturgy would come in useful one day,' said Doc.

'Yes, and that seminar we gave certainly seems to have done the generals some good,' observed Hairy. 'I doubt if we'll have any more trouble from them.'

'We can all sleep safely in our beds again,' added Dozey.

'Well, yes . . .,' commented Dopey, with a trace of irony in his voice as he remembered the first night that Snow White had come to stay.

Picking up his meaning, Grumpy followed on with, 'Just think how pleased Snow White will be that we've saved her!'

'Er, just a small point,' ventured Jock, 'but where exactly is she?'

Seven little looks of horror spread across the dwarfs' faces. Snow White was nowhere to be seen! They searched all around in great consternation, and then rushed to the Dark Tower to get a better view of the surrounding countryside. They climbed to the top, and peered out into the distance.

'There she is!' Dopey shouted. 'The evil queen has captured her, and is taking her towards that grove of trees!'

'Of course!' exclaimed Hairy. 'While we were all busy with the generals, the queen simply strode in and took Snow White away. Wherever is she taking her?'

'It will be the Deep Dungeons,' explained Doc, 'which are situated in that grove.'

'Quick, then, not a moment to lose!' shouted Bossy as they hurried to the bottom of the tower. 'We must get to the dungeons as quickly as we can!'

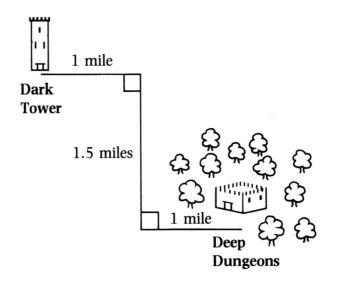

Now, this presented the dwarfs with a bit of a problem, because they had never made the journey from the Dark Tower to the Deep Dungeons before. They knew that they had two alternatives, as shown in the diagram: they could either run along the road, which took a zig-zag course turning through two right angles, or they could run the straight-line route across the fields, which would, however, be at a lesser speed. On the road, their speed in miles per hour would be one-fifth of the lowest number that is the sum of squares of positive whole numbers in two ways. Across the fields, their speed would be one-half of the lowest positive number that is the difference of the squares of positive whole numbers in two different ways.

So how long did it take the dwarfs to get to the Dungeons?

35   Freeing Snow White

The dwarfs arrived at the dungeons very out of breath, and soon traced Snow White's cries to a room deep underground. The evil queen had locked her in and returned to her palace, evidently intending to return and finish off her grisly deed.

The door was secured with seven locks, labelled A, B, C, D, E, F and G, and each appeared easy enough to undo. But Snow White warned them: 'Be careful! The locks have to be undone in a certain order, or this room will be flooded with melted chocolate!'

'Of course!' exclaimed Bossy. A distant memory had surfaced in his mind. 'Don't you remember, this was once part of a chocolate mine where we worked, before it was converted into the dungeons?' he said to the older dwarfs. They racked their brains to remember some information that would save Snow White from a sticky end.

Bossy could remember that F came before A in the code, and Hairy was able to add that C was more places before D than F was before A. Jock knew that G preceded F by even more places, and Doc remembered that E was ahead of D by more places still.

After much straining of their tiny intellects, the dwarfs came up with the correct combination, and successfully released Snow White. Overcome with relief, she gave them all a peck on the cheek, and their faces turned red with embarrassment. Then they wasted no more time in rushing back to the safety of their cottage.

What was the combination that released Snow White?

HAPPY EVER AFTER

36   The prince

'You're back early,' said the queen. 'Reviewing the troops usually takes longer than that.'

'There are usually more than seven of them, my dear,' replied the king.

'The generals were the only troops there. What has happened to the rest I cannot imagine. There used to be over ten thousand of them.'

The queen kept a poker face.

The king continued, 'And what made it all the more humiliating was that we have a prince visiting especially to see the ceremony.'

The prince in question, a very handsome young man, then entered. The king introduced him to the queen, and continued, 'I really must apologise for the fiasco. Things don't seem to have gone at all well recently, what with my lovely daughter going missing a few months ago.'

'That must have been heartbreaking for you both,' said the prince, considerately.

'Yes, the whole business affected me deeply,' replied the queen.

'Perhaps I could try to find her for you,' volunteered the prince. 'She is unlikely to have gone far.'

'That would be most kind of you,' said the king.

'Yes, it would,' added the queen. A plan had materialised in her mind, as she thought of all the beautiful princess and handsome prince stories she had heard lately. If the prince would take Snow White off her hands, the queen would again be the fairest in the land – admittedly it would not be as much fun for the queen that way, but all her assassination plans had failed. 'The best place for you to start is probably the woods – there are many places she could be lurking in there.'

Forthwith the prince set out, but when he reached them, he saw that the woods were a jumble of paths. In an attempt to search methodically, he decided to take specific turnings at junctions according to how many paths met there: first left when three paths met; first right when four paths met; second left when five paths met; second right when six paths met.

Following this strategy, he reached in succession junctions where the number of paths was 3, 5, 6, 4, 6, 3, 5, 4, 3, 6, 5, 3, 6, 3, 4, 6. After all that, his strategy led him to a little cottage.

Answering his knock, a beautiful young girl opened the door, announcing, 'The dwarfs' residence; may I help you?'

The prince was momentarily frozen by their mutual attraction, but stated his quest.

'Why, I am Snow White,' said the girl.

'At last!' cried the prince. 'After all those twisting paths and confusing junctions, some with four or five paths meeting.'

'But there is only one place where four paths meet, and only one where five meet,' said Snow White.

'In that case, I could probably have got here sooner,' replied the prince. How?

37   Wishful thinking

The dwarfs had been very encouraged by Snow White's show of gratitude after they had rescued her. Each of them therefore decided to buy her a present in the hope that his particular fantasy would be fulfilled.

The dwarf who wanted to hold hands with Snow White had bought her some chocolate.

The red tulips had been bought by the dwarf who wanted to look at Snow White from a distance.

Hairy hoped that if his gift of crocuses was acceptable, he would be able to take Snow White for a walk.

The dwarf who wanted to stroke Snow White's hair and who had bought her daisies was not Doc.

Jock was a dwarf of action and did not want to gaze into Snow White's eyes.

Dozey didn't want to sit with Snow White or look at her from a distance.

Grumpy was the only dwarf who had not bought flowers, while it was Bossy who had bought the daffodils.

None of the dwarfs whose name started with a D had bought freesias, or wanted to gaze into Snow White's eyes.

The dwarf who had bought violets didn't want to kiss Snow White and wasn't Dopey.

Snow White was delighted to receive her gifts and treated all the dwarfs fairly – as you would expect the fairest of them all to do – by ignoring them all and instead announcing her engagement to the handsome prince. The dwarfs had to look from a distance, which at least fulfilled the dreams of one of them.

Who was that, who bought the violets, and who wanted to kiss Snow White?

38   Who's who

'I'm going to have a cup of tea,' said Hairy. 'Who else wants one?'

'I do,' said Jock.

'I'd love one,' said Grumpy.

'Not for me, thanks,' said Doc.

'I'll have one,' said Bossy. 'So will Dopey when he gets back.'

Finally Dozey said, 'No, I won't, thank you.'

'Right, that's four,' said Hairy.

'Excuse me, I think you've made a mistake,' said the handsome prince. 'That makes five.'

Hairy looked at him in a knowing way. 'No, four,' he insisted, and proceeded to make enough tea for every dwarf who wanted some.

'Perhaps I can explain,' said Snow White to the prince. 'Every once in a while they have a day when each of the dwarfs must only make true statements, or only make false ones. They decide among themselves the night before, as to who will be truth-tellers and who will be liars. So the next day each of them knows who'll tell the truth and who'll lie, and it doesn't inconvenience them – but it makes things very complicated for anyone else!' Of course, Snow White wasn't part of this arrangement, so she was telling the truth.

'So some of the dwarfs were probably lying when they said they wanted tea?' asked the prince.

'That's right,' said Snow White, 'but Hairy will know exactly how much tea to make, because he and all the others know which ones were lying.'

'I wonder how many were lying,' the prince said.

Dopey had just come in, and he picked up the cup of tea that had been made for him. 'Either there are two lying dwarfs today, or there are two truth-telling ones,' he offered.

The prince tried to check this, by finding out who had had tea and comparing that with whether they had said they wanted tea, but by the time he got round to it he discovered that all the tea had been drunk.

Meanwhile Snow White went off to read a book that she saw lying on a table. 'Look at this,' she said to the prince after a while. 'It's a book that's got lots of puzzles and lots of stories about the dwarfs – and me as well,' she finished, blushing. 'And at the front of the book they all pretend to be other people,' she continued. 'Look at these strange names: Barry, Colin, Gordon, Ian, Keith, Martin, Neil. Each one of those names is another name for one of the dwarfs, but I've no idea which goes with which. I wonder if they could tell me.'

Bossy was the first to speak. 'Keith's dwarf-name has a D in it,' he said.

'Gordon's dwarf-name ends in Y,' said Jock.

'No, it doesn't,' said Grumpy. 'It's got a C or an E in it, though.'

Then Dopey stated, 'Hairy's other name is Ian.'

Doc said, 'I'm not Barry.'

Hairy chipped in with, 'Gordon's dwarf-name contains an R or a C.'

Snow White tried to gather her thoughts. 'So,' she said, 'they were all offered tea.'

'Martin had tea,' said Doc.

'Neil had tea,' said Dozey.

'And,' continued Snow White, 'some of them might be lying today.'

'Martin is lying today,' said Dopey.

'Neil and Barry are both lying today,' said Hairy.

'Finally,' concluded Snow White, 'each of the dwarfs has another, rather funny-sounding, name.'

'That's right,' said the handsome prince. 'So I wonder if we can work out which name goes with which dwarf.'

3 The isle of Maranga

THE NATION

39   The weather

The weather on the isle of Maranga covers the extremes. Over a year, they have five hot months, then two warm ones, then two cold ones, then three warm ones. As regards wind, they have three still months, then two breezy ones, then four windy ones, then three breezy ones. The precipitation pattern is that they get four showery months, then three wet ones, then three dry ones, then two wet ones. That is the regular pattern of how the weather varies with the calendar months, although those patterns don't necessarily all start on the same month, of course.

February is a month that sees very few tourists, because it is cold, showery and breezy. I personally find the dry, hot and windy month very oppressive; my favourite is the breezy, warm and dry one. Which month is that?

40   The population

Between 1902 and 1952 the population of Maranga increased by 30 000. Dividing up the population into adults and children, and males and females, the following information can be given about the number of men, women, boys and girls.

In 1902 the census showed that 60% of the people were males. There were half as many boys as females, and for every four boys there were three girls.

In the 1952 census, 25% of the total were children. The number of adults was five times the number of boys, and there were as many women as males. The number of children now equalled the number of females in 1902.

How many women were there in 1902, and how many in 1952?

41   The flag

The Maranga flag is very interesting. The standard size is 36 chisen long by 24 chisen high, and it is divided into three regions of equal area: one red, one white and one blue. Three straight lines separate the regions, all starting from a point that is five chisen from the hoist (the flagpole side) and nine chisen from the top; one of these lines goes to the top edge, one to the fly (the free edge), and one to the bottom edge, in all cases a whole number of chisen along the edge. What then are these three measurements in chisen?

42   St Tarnop's day

St Tarnop's day is the first Wednesday of the year that is the nth day of the nth month – say, 1 January or 2 February, and so on. However, this unusual arrangement means that in some years there is no St Tarnop's day at all. What is the longest interval there can be between St Tarnop's days, and when did this last occur?

43   Traffic lights

In Maranga they drive on the left, but the traffic lights take a bit of getting used to. They have four colours – orange, turquoise, puce and violet – which correspond (in some order) to four meanings:

(a)   You may proceed in any direction.
(b)   You may go left or straight, and may go right if there is nothing coming towards you.
(c)   You may go left.
(d)   Stop.

The combinations of colours that can occur are, of course, sensibly chosen, so that two cars wanting to cross each other's paths aren't both allowed to proceed.

So, for instance, you could see at crossroads the arrangements of lights shown in the two diagrams. The diagrams also show eight cars 1, 2, . . ., 8 waiting to travel in the directions indicated. The set of traffic lights governing the movement of each car is positioned to the *car's* left. Which of the cars can proceed?

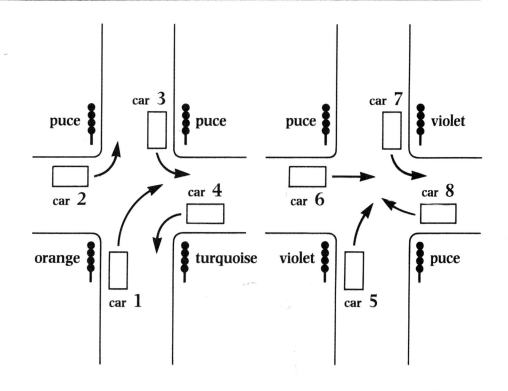

44   Signposts

Some of the villages in the remoter parts of Maranga are rather poorly signposted. Measures are being taken to improve this, and on a recent visit I saw signposts being made for eight neighbouring villages, showing their interconnections. The roads do not cross anywhere except in the village centres, and these are the sites where the signposts will stand.

When I saw them, each signpost was complete except for one name, and there was no indication which signpost would be placed in which village. The names on each signpost, in clockwise order with the missing one last, were:

1.   Gyra, Spranso, Blimpscoe, –
2.   Tuvo, –
3.   Gyra, Aytow, –
4.   Tuvo, Aytow, Blimpscoe, –
5.   Cellawa, Spranso, –
6.   Rackle, –
7.   Wertso, Blimpscoe, –
8.   Tuvo, Rackle, –

Which signpost will stand in which village, and what are the missing names?

THE SIGHTS

45   The Palace

The Royal Palace is situated in Pitalca. It has many rooms, and each has only one window. The rooms are numbered in a logical manner: 1, 2, 3, 4, etc. From the outside of the building, the windows make a colourful sight, for no two are identical, as they have four characteristics that can be varied.

The shapes of the windows follow the pattern: square, circular, arched, rectangular, lancet, square, circular, and so on. These are glazed such that six have plain glass, then six have frosted glass, then the next six plain glass, and so on. Thus room 1 has a square window with plain glass, room 5 has a lancet window with plain glass, and room 9 has a rectangular window with frosted glass.

Four types of drape are used and these follow the sequence: venetian blind, curtains, net, roller blind, . . .; their colours follow the sequence: red, orange, yellow, green, blue, black, white, red, orange, yellow, . . ., each sequence going by room number.

The Palace has as many rooms as it could possibly have under these conditions, given that no two windows appear alike. What is the number of rooms? And if the blue net curtains in the room with circular frosted windows are exchanged with the green curtains from the room numbered one lower, for which room numbers will the windows now appear identical?

46 The chimes

The magnificent chimes of the Great Clock adjoining the Palace are a stirring sound. On the hours, the ten chimes consist of an arrangement of the four bells rung singly, and the six combinations of a pair of bells rung simultaneously. In musical terms, the whole peal can be thought of as three bars each having six beats, with the ten chimes being two semibreves (four beats each), two minims (two beats), two dotted crotchets (one and a half beats), two crotchets (one beat) and two quavers (half a beat).

The first three chimes get progressively shorter; the last five chimes get progressively longer, as do chimes three to five. The peal starts with bells B and D together, and ends with bells A and C together. Bell A is not rung in the first bar; the fourth chime includes bell B; and when bell A is rung on its own it follows another single bell. No bell is ever rung twice in succession. What is the full peal?

47 The Great Hall

In the Great Hall of the Palace the floor is covered with a pattern of wood blocks. There is one central regular octagon, representing the Sun, and the rest are identical shapes representing the Royal Crown. The diagram shows the octagon with one of the crown shapes in place. All the sides of the octagon and the crown shape are the same length, and all the angles are multiples of 45°. The pattern is cut off at the walls, but it could extend for ever. What does the full pattern look like?

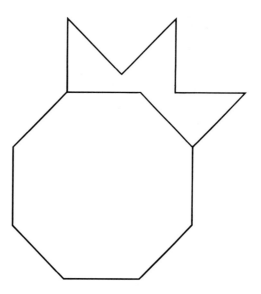

48   The courtyard

The diagram shows a picture of the courtyard of the Palace at Pitalca. The courtyard is paved with fifteen large rectangular slabs, each consisting of two patterned squares. Each individual square has one of five patterns on it, and no two paving slabs are identical. Please identify how each slab is laid.

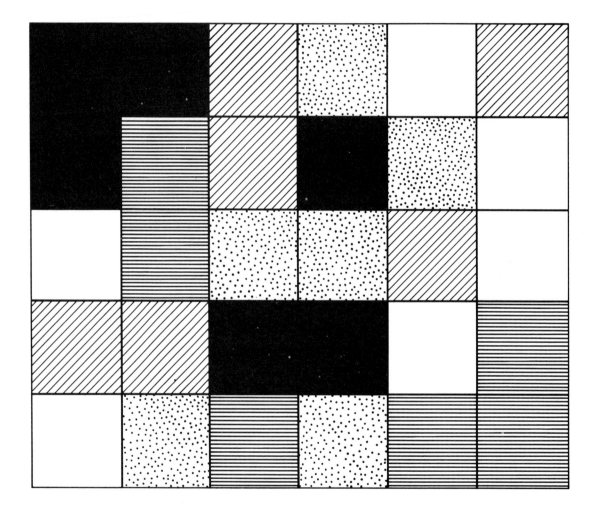

49   The park

Behind the Palace is the park, which is nine grunolfs by seven grunolfs, but with four sections missing from the corners, each one grunolf by two grunolfs. There is a lake, one grunolf square, the nearer edges being two grunolfs from the north boundary and three grunolfs from the west. All this is shown in the plan.

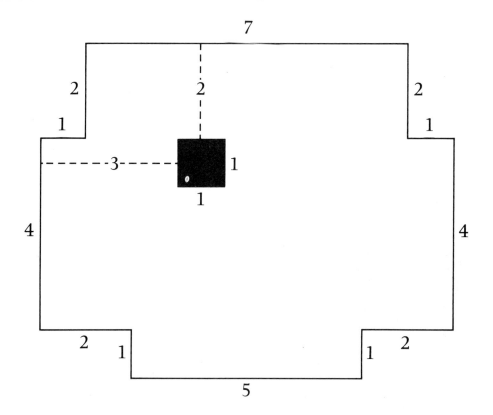

A narrow path leads from the edge of the park to the lake, splits to go round both sides of the lake along the edges, rejoins and then leads to the edge of the park again. In this way it divides the park (excluding the lake) into two parts, and it does so in such a way that the two parts are exactly the same shape. What is the route of the path?

50   The castle

The castle in Pitalca is an interesting shape. Its outer walls are straight, each meets its two neighbours in a right angle, and they form a complete circuit. The lengths of the walls are 3, 4, 5, 5, 5, 8, 8, 8, 12 and 20 mathofs, in some order, and the area enclosed is 124 square mathofs. What is the shape?

UNITS

51 The currency

Decimalization has not yet reached Maranga. The unit of currency is the arpep, which is subdivided into versils, which in turn can be split into precops. One pound sterling at the current exchange rate is worth 1 arpep 11 versils 7 precops, so that for £100 you would get 139 arpeps 19 versils 18 precops. If you pay for an item costing 5 arpeps 24 versils 17 precops with a 7 arpep note, what change will you receive, and how much is the item worth in sterling?

52 Small change

I still haven't learnt to recognize the Marangan coinage. Recently, I was given four coins in change totalling 28 precops, and on another occasion I received five coins totalling 21 precops. All I noticed was that each time I got the same three denominations of coin, each obviously a whole number of precops. What were these three coins worth?

53 Lengths and areas

I recently stayed on an estate in Maranga. The land-owner told me that it was an exact square in shape. He did tell me the length of the side in grunolfs and mathofs, and what the area was, but all I can remember is that it was a whole number of square grunolfs (fewer than 2000) plus 1770 square mathofs. There are certainly fewer than 5000 square mathofs in a square grunolf, though. What was the size of my acquaintance's estate, and how many mathofs are there in a grunolf?

LEGENDS

54 Journeys of St Tarnop

There are many tales of the journeys of St Tarnop, during which he had many adventures. It is only recently that historians have agreed on a consistent set of stories, which together might solve the long-standing riddle of where Tarnop was buried. The old map of Maranga shown here gives the agreed positions of the villages and other features in Tarnop's time. The precise location of each feature is halfway along the bottom of the symbol (except for the asymmetrical mountain symbol, in which case it is the point on the bottom immediately below the highest peak).

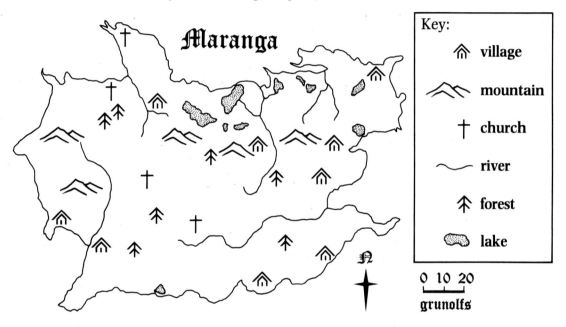

The tales tell that Tarnop was born of humble parentage in a remote area due south of a mountain, and due east of a church. When he grew to a youth, he travelled north-east to a village, where he lived for a number of years, learning skills and quietly doing noble deeds. Eventually, the time had come for him to travel again, and he set off due west until he reached a river, which he followed to its source. He spent many years in this area before moving directly to the nearest forest, where he lived a simple, contemplative life. In his later years he became more active, and made his home on the shore of a lake 70 grunolfs away. When he sensed that his end was near, he headed towards the nearest village, but died and was buried 10 grunolfs short of it.

Can you help the scholars establish where he was buried, and how many grunolfs he travelled on these journeys?

55   Hastaman's gifts

One particular legend of St Tarnop, and perhaps the most enduring of all, tells how he overthrew the evil dominion of Hastaman and Heobard.

These two had held the land in terror for many years, in a very cunning way. Hastaman would frequently visit the hapless citizens, pretending kindness and lavishing more and more gifts upon them, which they dared not refuse. Heobard would then visit everyone each year, demanding that they prove they still had all the gifts, and exacting dreadful punishment on anyone who could not account for them.

For a favoured few, Hastaman had a special plan. There were six items with charmed properties, namely amulets, bangles, chalices, drakestones, emblems and flagons. Certain sets of these taken together would give the owner magical powers. In order to tantalize the favoured few but still burden them as much as possible, Hastaman kept giving each person different charmed items, until he could give no more without letting that person have a magical set. In this way, the possible groups of items that he could let one of the favoured few own were:

amulet, bangle, emblem;
amulet, bangle, flagon;
amulet, chalice, emblem;
amulet, chalice, flagon;
amulet, drakestone, emblem;
bangle, chalice, drakestone;
bangle, chalice, emblem;
bangle, chalice, flagon;
bangle, drakestone, flagon;
chalice, drakestone, emblem;
chalice, drakestone, flagon;
emblem, flagon.

Hastaman could quickly check whether a set was magical, because he had a list of what were known as the mystical sets. These sets were those magical sets which would not be magical if any of the items were removed. A set was then magical precisely when it contained a mystical set (or was itself mystical).

What were the mystical sets?

56   Tarnop and Hastaman

Eventually Tarnop saw that the land could take the oppression no more. He was not one of the favoured few, but he boldly marched to Hastaman's vault and demanded to be included. 'Very well,' said Hastaman, and placed one of each charmed item on a table in front of him. 'You may select which items you will own, but we shall proceed in this wise. First, you shall choose an item, and then I will remove one, and then you shall choose one of the remainder, and so on in alternation.'

Tarnop considered carefully, and then chose his first item. The selection then proceeded, but the outcome was inevitable; after Tarnop's first choice, Hastaman could not prevent him obtaining a magical set. Invested with such power, he then advanced on Hastaman and swiftly despatched him.

Which item had Tarnop chosen first?

57   Tarnop and Heobard

Following his defeat of Hastaman, Tarnop returned home to prepare for the inevitable battle with Heobard. It is said that Heobard was one of the mightiest fighters who ever lived in the land of Maranga. The only protection that Tarnop could obtain was a shield.

This shield had been forged in the dim dawn of history, and was made up of a number of pieces of metal all of different sizes welded together. The shield had a magical quality, as the areas of these individual pieces formed a consecutive sequence of prime numbers, with a total area of less than 1000 units.

The fight began. The first stroke of Heobard's mighty sword resounded on the shield, and pieces representing one half of the area fell to the ground. A second stroke, and again metal representing half the remaining area was lost. A third swing, and once more half the remaining area fell to the ground. With only a small shield left, Tarnop had to use all his skill to avoid the fourth blow, and this time three-quarters of the area that had been left fell to the floor. With Tarnop left holding a single piece of the original shield, both men momentarily looked bemused; then Tarnop dashed in and, with a short stabbing motion, killed the tyrant.

What was the size of the last piece of the shield, and what were the areas of the pieces that fell on the second stroke?

HISTORY

58   King Nogdor

The first king of all Maranga was Nogdor, and he came to the throne in his twenties. On his succession and each anniversary of it, his loyal subjects made him a crown, with one jewel in it for every year of his age. His reign ended in his forties, just before one of his anniversaries, and by that time the total number of jewels in all the crowns was at least 680, although not as many as 690. How many years did Nogdor reign?

59   King Olnic

Nogdor was succeeded by Olnic, who on his succession instituted three courts – the Archdukes', the Barons' and the Commoners' – which met that year and at regular intervals thereafter. The intervals differed from court to court, being three, five and eight years, but historical records are not clear on which court met at which interval.

When Olnic had been reigning for a good many years, but had no obvious heir, the Archdukes' court on one of their meetings gave consideration to the matter of succession. They resolved to ask for recommendations from the Barons, when their court next met; the Barons in turn sought advice from the Commoners' court at its next meeting. Following this, on their next meeting the Barons' court considered the proposed names, and passed some of them forward for a final decision by the next Archdukes' court.

Unfortunately, it happened that each time a request or information went from one court, the next had only just met the previous year, so that the delay was longer than it might have been. The very day before the Archdukes' court was to meet, the grand old king passed away, and the succession was in confusion. How many years had Olnic reigned?

60 King Hetik

The throne was then seized by Hetik, but his position was always uncertain, as rival claimants gathered their forces. He once asked a soothsayer to tell him how long he would reign, and received the reply, 'A number of years and a number of days, your majesty; and if you square that number of days, it will give you the total length of your reign in days.'

This calculation was never solved by the palace mathematicians, who were still struggling with the Gregorian calendar, which had been introduced just before the reign started. Hetik saw the island into the eighteenth century (and the mathematicians correctly instructed people that 1700 was not a leap year), but he was deposed by an uprising on the last day of 1702. For how many years and how many days had he reigned?

61 Civil wars

From the beginning of 1703 until the end of 1845 there was unrest and confusion on the island. Three separate warring houses – Eresord, Beresoul and Switheroe – fought over the crown. Between them there were five continuous periods when one of the houses held control, and after the battles the new reigning house always officially started on the first day of the year.

The confusion that the ordinary citizens felt was worsened by the fact that the three houses each had a different dating system: Eresord dates were 102 years behind our normal dates, Beresoul dates were nine years ahead of our dates, and Switheroe dates were 60 years ahead of ours.

Events during this period of turmoil are often referred to by the dates of the then ruling house. Amazingly, though, there is no ambiguity in doing this, because each of the 143 years of the strife in our dating is represented exactly once with this system; it is just that they are rearranged. What, in their system and ours, were the dates of the various houses?

62   Modern kings

At the beginning of 1846, the situation stabilized. An acceptable solution was found whereby the houses of Eresord, Beresoul and Switheroe united to form the modern Maranga dynasty.

The first such king was Tramin, who ruled for 33 years and was succeeded by his son. Another Tramin was also succeeded by his own son, but himself followed his own brother, and ruled for 23 years. One king Ani succeeded his own brother and reigned for 8 years, and the other followed his own father and reigned for 3 years, but they were both succeeded by their own brothers. King Rybar succeeded his own father, and was followed by an Ani after a reign of 14 years.

Even with this repetition of names, no two brothers bore the same name, of course. One king Elni ruled for 11 years after his brother, and was succeeded by another Elni. An Elni also succeeded the Elni who reigned for 17 years after his own father. The Elni who followed his own brother's son enjoyed a reign of 23 years, and was succeeded by his own brother. The current king is also an Elni, and he succeeded his own father.

What are the dates of these nine kings?

MUSIC

If you are at all interested in music, you will find that the island has a character all its own. It owes a lot to European influence, with the chromatic scale of twelve notes a semitone apart forming an octave (say C, C♯, D, D♯, E, F, F♯, G, G♯, A, A♯, B, and then the cycle repeating), but the traditional instruments are unique adaptations of ones familiar to us. With a little exploring, you will be able to find these fascinating instruments being played in atmospheric surroundings.

63   The rituga

The rituga is a stringed and fretted instrument. There are four strings, which may be strummed open to give the basic note, or stopped at any of the frets, each of which raises the pitch of the note by a semitone. For instance, the four notes of a D7 chord – namely, D, F♯, A and C – can be sounded by stopping the first, second, third and fourth strings at the seventh, fifth, seventh and fifth frets respectively. (Therefore, the pitch of the first string open, plus seven semitones, must be one of those four notes, and each of those four notes occurs once with that fingering.) Equally, the four notes of a G6 chord – namely, G, B, D and E – can be sounded by leaving the first string open, stopping the third and fourth strings at the second and third frets respectively, and . . . stopping the second string at which fret?

64   The prettum

The prettum is a valved brass instrument. Three keys operate the valves, so that each key can independently raise the pitch of a note by a certain number of semitones. With no keys depressed, the basic pitch is obtained; with all three keys depressed, the note an octave (i.e. twelve semitones) above it is obtained. With the eight possible fingerings (including, of course, these two), eight consecutive notes from the scale of C major (which contains just the notes A, B, C, D, E, F and G) can be sounded, but not necessarily going from C to the C one octave above. What, then, is the lowest note?

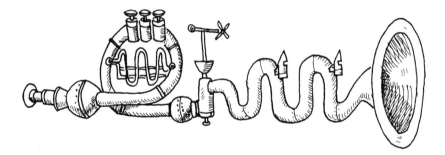

65   The parahout

The parahout is a very easy instrument to play. It consists of a number of open strings, and a number of dampers that may be pressed onto them. Each damper cuts out a number of the notes, and allows the rest to sound, and the pattern is repeated for each octave (so that, say, either all the Gs are cut out by a damper, or none is cut out by it). By depressing pairs of dampers, and strumming across all the strings, all the undamped strings can be made to sound and so produce a chord. For instance, dampers 1 and 2 together allow the chord of C major to sound (the notes being C, E and G); dampers 2 and 3 together allow A major to sound (the notes are A, C♯ and E), while dampers 1 and 3 together allow a major chord to sound (the intervals between the notes of a major chord being four, three and five semitones in that order). Dampers 3 and 4 together produce a diminished chord (intervals are three, three, three and three semitones), and dampers 2 and 4 together result in a minor sixth (intervals are three, four, two and three semitones). Dampers 1 and 4 together would allow which notes to sound?

66   The grano

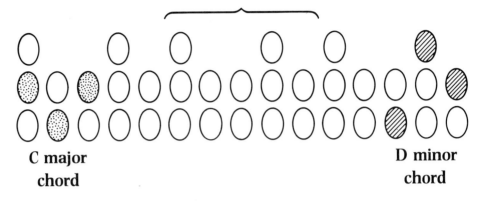

The grano is a large keyboard instrument, with a very unusual pattern of keys, as shown in the diagram. There are two full rows of keys and one partial row, and between them all the notes are represented once each, over a number of octaves. Within each row (even the partial one) the keys from left to right produce increasingly high notes, and at any position the note in the middle row is higher than that in the bottom row, and if there is a note in the top row at that position then that is higher still. The basic pattern of notes in the group of twelve shown is repeated along the keyboard, up by successive octaves to the right and down by successive octaves to the left.

The diagram also shows how you can play the notes of a C major chord (C, E and G, but maybe in an inversion, i.e. not necessarily in that increasing order); the three keys for this are shown shaded, at the low end of the keyboard. At the high end of the keyboard some more shading shows how to achieve the notes of a D minor chord (D, F and A, again not necessarily in that order). So, what is the arrangement of notes within the basic pattern?

4 The Martian dating agency and other problems

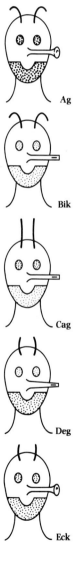

Ag

Bik

Cag

Deg

Eck

MARTIANS

67 The Martian dating agency

The largest dating agency on Mars needs some assistance with a final bit of sorting out. They have selected a group of fifteen Martians – five of each sex – who have very similar interests, and it just remains to arrange them into five triples according to their preferences for physical characteristics, if that's martianly possible.

Now, you do know about Martian biology, don't you? No? Didn't your nuther teach you about the birds, the bees and the bloopnids? No? Here we go, then. There are three sexes, male, female and numale, and the adults are easily distinguished by their facial fur – males have beards, females have manes, and numales have crests. This fur can be coloured yellow, pink or violet. Each face has two peepers, which can be coloured red, blue or green. Each face also has two antennae, which can be shaped as short, droopy or long. Finally, each face has a hooter, which can be shaped as flat, tapering or flared.

The illustrations show pictures of the fifteen clients, and the files show the relevant details. All you have to do is to sort them into triples, one of each sex, so that everyone's preference is met. May I wish you all the luck on the planet!

Males

Name	Peepers	Hooter	Fur	Antennae	Preference
Ag	blue	flared	violet	droopy	female's peepers not blue
Bik	green	flat	yellow	droopy	numale's fur not pink
Cag	red	flat	yellow	tall	two partners have same colour fur
Deg	green	tapering	pink	short	numale's antennae not tall
Eck	red	flared	pink	short	female's fur not yellow

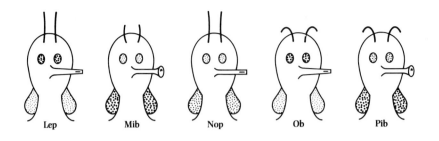

Females

Name	Peepers	Hooter	Fur	Antennae	Preference
Lep	blue	tapering	yellow	tall	male's fur not violet
Mib	green	flared	violet	short	numale's antennae not short
Nop	green	flat	pink	tall	numale's peepers not red
Ob	blue	tapering	yellow	droopy	two partners have different-shaped hooters
Pib	red	flared	violet	droopy	male's fur not pink

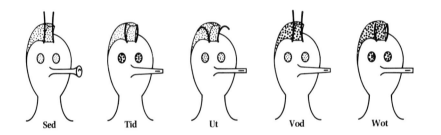

Numales

Name	Peepers	Hooter	Fur	Antennae	Preference
Sed	green	flared	pink	tall	male's peepers not red
Tid	blue	tapering	yellow	short	male's hooter not flared
Ut	red	flat	pink	droopy	male's antennae not tall
Vod	red	tapering	violet	tall	female's hooter not flared
Wot	blue	flat	violet	short	female's hooter not flat

68   Martian genetics

Having learnt a little about Martian biology, you may well wonder how facial characteristics are passed from one generation to the next. Intense study by geneticists has revealed that, although Martian reproduction is a complicated procedure, the genetic characteristics can be summarized in a simple table:

Characteristic	Genetic score		
	0	1	2
Sex	male	female	numale
Peepers	red	green	blue
Hooter	flat	tapering	flared
Fur	violet	pink	yellow
Antennae	long	short	droopy

At conception, one of the three parents has double the contribution of the other two. So to find a particular characteristic of a newborn Martian, add up the genetic scores for the male, female and numale parents, doubling the appropriate score; then, if necessary, take off multiples of 3 until the score is one of 0, 1 or 2. This then gives the genetic score for the offspring, and the table can be used to translate the number into the particular characteristic.

For instance, suppose that the father has green peepers, the mother blue, and the nuther also blue, and that the numale provided the dominant contribution. Then the sex of the offspring scores $0 + 1 + 2 \times 2 = 5$, which reduces to 2, i.e. numale; the score for the peepers is $1(\text{green}) + 2(\text{blue}) + 2 \times 2(\text{blue}) = 7$, which reduces to 1, i.e. green.

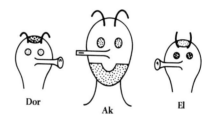

Dor Ak El

You will see a delightful picture of a proud father with two of his children. You'll notice that facial fur on children appears always the same, as a circular patch; this moults when adulthood is reached, and is replaced by a beard, mane or crest as appropriate. Although endings of adults' names indicate their sex, children's names fail to do so, because the ending changes at adulthood.

You will have noted that Ak has red peepers, a flat hooter, pink fur and droopy antennae, while Dor has green peepers, a flared hooter, violet fur and droopy antennae, and El has blue peepers, a flared hooter, yellow fur and short antennae. Given that the mother's antennae are not long, what are the facial characteristics of the mother and nuther (Bep and Ced), and what are the sexes of Dor and El?

69   Martian dancing

The dance that is currently sweeping Mars is the whirltz, a strictly rhythmical, close-contact dance that is fun to learn. It's always a social asset to learn to dance, so why not study these simple rules, and soon you could be invited to all the most elegant Martian parties.

Participants

The dance is performed by couples, one numale and one female. The numale and female face each other at all times.

Framework

The positions of feet (at the beginning and end of each step) are points on a triangular grid.

The numale's right foot and left foot must both be adjacent on the grid to its middle foot. (You hadn't forgotten that Martians have three feet, had you?) Similarly for the female.

At the end of each step, each of the numale's feet must be adjacent on the grid to at least one of the female's, and vice versa.

These rules thus determine a limited number of allowable positions, not counting rotations and translations.

Steps

The numale moves forwards, and the female moves backwards, in two sorts of step; or the numale stays still but lifts its partner sideways, in the third sort.

In the first sort of step the numale moves one of its feet onto the grid point occupied by one of the female's feet, while the female moves that foot to a new point. These steps are designated L, M or R according as it is the numale's left, middle or right foot that moves.

In the second sort of step the numale moves one of its feet onto the grid point occupied by one of the female's feet, while the female moves that foot and one other to new points. These steps are designated G or D according as it is the numale's left or right foot that moves.

In the third sort of step the numale does not move any of its feet, but the female moves all three, each by one grid position. These steps are designated A or O according as the female moves to the numale's left or right.

From a given position, not all of these steps will be possible.

Dance

An A step may not be cancelled out by being followed immediately by an O step, nor vice versa.

The dance consists of four-step and eight-step patterns. Each of these patterns begins with the same step. There are thus eight possible eight-step patterns in which the numale moves forwards two 'paces'.

Similarly there are two possible four-step patterns in which the numale turns 60° left (about one of its feet). Equally there are two possible four-step patterns in which the numale turns 60° right (about one of its feet).

Exercises

Ready now? The music is starting!

For today's lesson, could you just show one pattern in which the numale goes forward, one in which it turns left, and one in which it turns right?

70   Martian sport

While Martian females and numales get exercise from dancing, there's nothing the average male likes better than an invigorating game of taildisc. While we needn't go into the rules of this intriguing game, the important point is that it involves three teams being on the pitch simultaneously.

Name	Peepers	Hooter	Fur	Antennae
Aik	green	flared	pink	droopy
Bak	green	flat	yellow	droopy
Cug	red	flared	violet	droopy
Dak	blue	tapering	violet	long
Eeg	green	flat	yellow	long
Feg	green	flared	violet	short
Gok	red	flat	pink	short
Hig	blue	tapering	pink	droopy
Ick	green	flat	yellow	short
Jeg	red	flared	violet	short
Kig	red	flared	violet	long
Lek	blue	tapering	pink	droopy

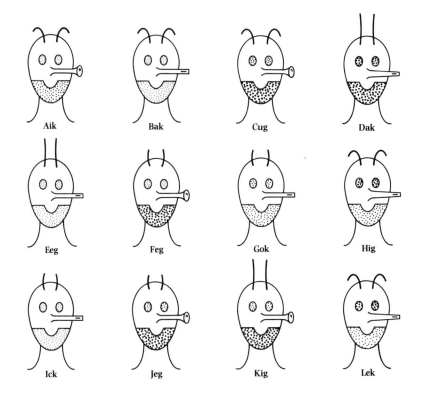

The twelve strapping males you see in the illustration have turned up for a friendly flickabout at the game, but they first have to pick sides. It would be most helpful if you could divide them up into three teams of four, so that all the members of a team have a common characteristic. (For example, one team consists of four of the five green-peepered males, all of another team have flat hooters, and all of the other team have flared hooters – except, of course, that that arrangement doesn't work.)

ARRANGEMENTS

71   Girls' school

It's very hard to keep track of who's friends with whom at the local girls' school, but I can tell you about ten of the girls.

Miss Nicholas is friends with Colette, Florence, Hazel and Isabel.

Miss O'Neill is friends with Ellen, Isabel and Joanna.

Miss Phillips is friends with Colette, Florence, Geraldine and Isabel.

Miss Qureshi is friends with Alison, Bronwen, Doris, Hazel and Joanna.

Miss Raje is friends with Florence, Geraldine and Isabel.

Miss Sewell is friends with Bronwen, Colette, Ellen, Hazel and Joanna.

Miss Tan is friends with Doris, Geraldine and Hazel.

Miss Uddin is friends with Alison, Ellen, Geraldine and Isabel.

Miss Victor is friends with Bronwen, Doris, Ellen and Joanna.

Miss Williams is friends with Alison, Florence and Geraldine.

What are the full names of all the girls?

72   Three over the eight

Eleven people went to the pub for a celebration drink. However, no two people had the same drinking habits, and in the space of two hours they all consumed different whole numbers of pints, ranging from one to eleven.

Dave sank twice as much as Edward. Frances downed three more than the less thirsty Irene. Lucy knocked back fewer than six pints, while Catherine was five behind Bill. Bill and Irene both liked a few jars, and stacked up more than six pints each. Gary lost count but was certain that he had more than Lucy. Kevin finished three times as much as Henry, who arrived late after going to the wrong pub. Catherine could only manage half as much as Alice, and Lucy's glass count was four less than Edward's.

Who drank exactly six pints?

73   Pop charts

I often listen to my local pop music station, particularly the chart programme. Each week they list the five current favourite records, and I usually note these down.

Now, I don't know if you've thought about it, but pop records in charts generally follow a particular pattern of behaviour – there's a period when they go up or stay the same each week, followed by a period when they go down or stay the same. It's quite rare for a record to fluctuate and break this pattern.

I've recently come across notes I'd made of seven consecutive weeks of the chart, and I'd remarked that in that period exactly two of the records failed to show that regular behaviour. Unfortunately, I hadn't written down the dates of the charts (except that week V was in 1988 and week X was in 1989), so I don't know which order the charts came in, or which were the two 'irregular' records. Can you help me?

Week T
1. Killing time
2. Frenzy
3. Back in line
4. Loose talk
5. Maximum effect

Week U
1. Killing time
2. Just being there
3. Nobody else
4. Back in line
5. Go if you have to

Week V
1. Don't ask
2. I stand alone
3. Maximum effect
4. Back in line
5. Killing time

Week W
1. Nobody else
2. Even when you try
3. Children of hope
4. Back in line
5. Killing time

Week X
1. Nobody else
2. Even when you try
3. Maximum effect
4. Hard and fast
5. Back in line

Week Y
1. Killing time
2. Nobody else
3. Frenzy
4. Back in line
5. Even when you try

Week Z
1. Maximum effect
2. Don't ask
3. Another time maybe
4. Even when you try
5. Back in line

NUMBERS

74 Guastata gateau

The latest frozen gateau to reach the market is the Guastata gateau. It consists of a cuboid of crunchy carrot crumble (whose sides measured in centimetres are all integers), topped by a four centimetre layer of piquant prune purée. The whole is enrobed in a one centimetre layer of silky strawberry sorbet, forming a gateau which is longer than it is high. The sorbet represents one-half of the gateau by volume, while the purée is one-fifth of the gateau by volume. What are the dimensions of the Guastata gateau?

75 Birthday past

I once met somebody on her birthday who told me that the year was equal to the product of her parents' ages then; what was more, when she was born the year was equal to twice the product of her parents' ages then. In what year did I meet her, and how old was she then?

76 Calculator sum

A schoolboy was doing a simple sum of the form $(a+b)/c$, for which he knew the answer should have been 5. When he used his calculator, he pressed keys for $a+b/c=$ and got the answer 11. Thinking there might be something wrong with the calculator, he decided to check by changing the order of the addition. This time he pressed $b+a/c=$ and got the answer 14. What were the three numbers he was using, and given that there were no brackets on the calculator and he didn't want to type in any number twice, what keys should he have pressed to get the right answer?

77 Coded sums

The letters A to M represent the digits 1 to 9 and the arithmetic signs $+$, $-$, $\times$ and $/$; O is zero. Equations 1 to 6 each contain at least one sign, and arithmetic signs always have numbers on either side of them.

1. $G = GGHKK$
2. $DO = CFBA$
3. $KOO = ABDOBCF$
4. $ID = DJD$
5. $AM = MJM$
6. $L = IFHA$

What, in letters, is the answer to $CMEC$?

78   High score

Multiply together a number (at least two) of different prime numbers to yield a four-digit number N. The 'score' for this number N is the sum of the prime numbers used minus twenty times the sum of the first and third digits. (For example, $2537 = 43 \times 59$, so it has the score $43 + 59 - [20 \times (2 + 3)] = 2$.) Find the number N that gives the highest possible score when: (a) any primes may be used; (b) only primes less than 100 may be used.

PATTERNS

79   Onimods

With two colours, there are six essentially different ways of quartering a square and colouring the four sub-squares. These are shown in the first diagram, and we shall call them 'onimods'.

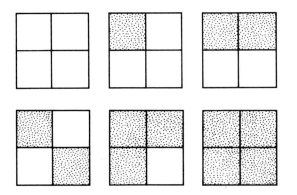

You have to form these 'onimods' into a 3×2 rectangle: three columns and two rows. As opposed to dominoes, onimods must 'clash' rather than match when they meet along an edge. So the possible meetings are as shown in the second diagram.

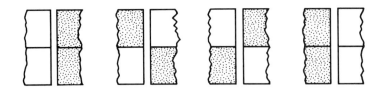

There are a few ways to form the rectangle. To solve the problem, though, you have to find the one which:

(a) has dark sub-squares in the top right and bottom left;
(b) does not have the same number of dark sub-squares in the top and bottom halves;
(c) has more dark sub-squares than light ones in the left third.

80   Sea horse

There's nothing that Sandy Paston likes more than riding her horse along the beach. Unfortunately, the tide's coming in and soon there will be no sand left.

A diagram of the area is shown below. Sandy's horse prances about on it like a chess knight. What with the rising tide, though, once the horse has landed on a square, the sand will become so soft that he can't land there again. And, as the tide rises, the squares gradually get covered with water, and therefore can't be used. The sand is rather uneven, and the squares are at different heights. All those marked with a 1 become engulfed just after the tenth move, all those with a 2 disappear just after the twentieth move, and so on.

Naturally, Sandy wants to go for as long a ride as possible, without getting stranded, so she must return to the starting square, which is marked with an asterisk.

What is the longest ride you can find?

4	2	2	1	2	1	6	3
6	1	5	3	5	3	4	1
6	3	5	4	6	1	2	6
2	2	4	1	3	1	2	5
6	4	5	2	3	6	1	4
1	3	6	7	3	4	6	5
5	6	7	5	3	4	5	2
*	1	2	5	7	3	4	4

81   Road map

The map shows the relative positions of nine towns: Keyton, Lutton, Manton, Newton, Pinton, Quarton, Ruffton, Senton and Teason. The distance between each pair of adjacent towns is also shown, in kilometres. Unfortunately, the map-maker has left the names of the towns off the grid, but luckily we have the following information about the distances between some of the towns. (Each distance means the shortest distance by a suitable choice of roads.)

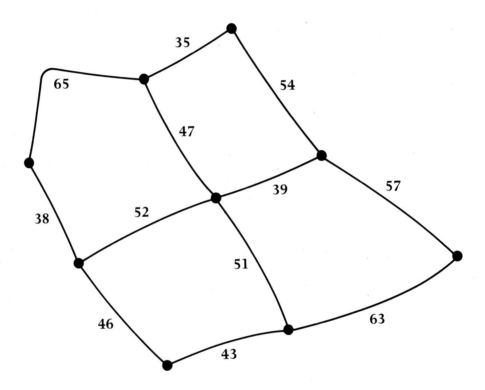

The two towns that are furthest apart are Senton and Keyton.

The distance from Senton to Quarton is the same as the distance from Teason to Manton.

The distance from Pinton to Newton is one kilometre more than the distance from Pinton to Manton.

The distance from Quarton to Ruffton is twice the distance from Quarton to Pinton.

Please label the map with the towns in their correct places.

82   Building a wall

You have a collection of bricks with which you have to build a wall ten courses high, in a pattern that repeats horizontally every twenty units. All bricks must be laid horizontally; in drawing out your solution, you need of course only show a basic repeating pattern that takes up twenty units each course, using a whole number of bricks, with the courses staggered as desired.

In the basic pattern you must use the following quantities of bricks of various lengths: one of length 14; three of length 12; three of length 10; six of length 8; eight of length 6; four of length 4; four of length 2.

This in itself is not too difficult, but in building your wall you must watch for potential 'cracks'. A 'crack' is a zig-zag line between bricks, extending from the top to the bottom (with vertical sections between adjacent bricks in the same course, and horizontal sections between adjacent courses). If the mortar weakens, this is how cracks would appear.

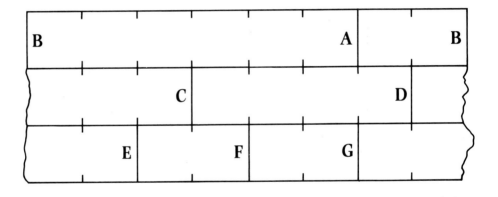

For instance, in the low wall shown in the diagram (with three courses and a repeating pattern horizontally every eight units, the pattern being $6+2$, $4+4$ and $4+2+2$ units respectively), the meetings of bricks within the courses are labelled A, B, ..., G, and 'cracks' can be identified by BCF or ADE, say. The 'length' of a crack is the sum of the horizontal distances (vertical distances are common to all cracks); so BCF has length $3+1=4$, ADE has length $1+3=4$, ADG has length $1+1=2$, and BDG has length $1+1=2$. These last two are the shortest for this low wall.

What you have to do is build a wall with the conditions first described, for which the shortest crack is as long as possible.

83   A coded maze

The maze shown must be done from left to right. The only way to leave the maze on reaching the exit is to give the password, the parts of which must be collected along your path and then decoded. Only the numbers along the shortest path are used (so no U-turns or unnecessary loops), and these are then multiplied together to produce the coded password. You will notice that the signs at the entrance and exit are written in the same code, but they are not part of the password.

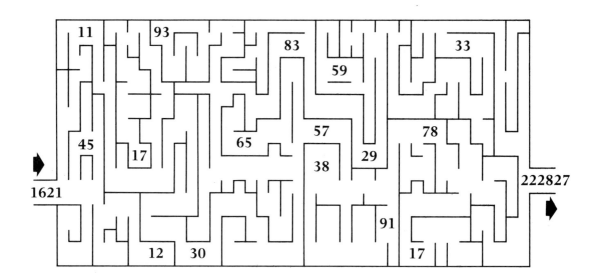

84   Steeplechasers

Horst Rayner is exercising some steeplechasers. They are good jumpers, but they tend to pull to the right a bit, and he has got to get them round a difficult course as quickly as possible.

The best way to understand the problem is to consider the horses to be like knights on a chessboard. The moves are similar, but they can only turn clockwise, and can only move if there is another horse to jump over. The horse jumped over is not, though, removed from the board. Put another way, a horse can only move if there is another horse adjacent to it (horizontally or vertically), and then its move can be thought of as one square onto the neighbouring horse, one square beyond, and then one square to the right. This is illustrated in the first diagram.

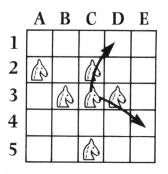

Possible moves from C3 are shown:

C3 to D1 is legal.
C3 to E4 is legal.
C3 to B5 is not legal, because there is no piece at C4 to jump over.
C3 to A2 is not legal, because A2 is already occupied.

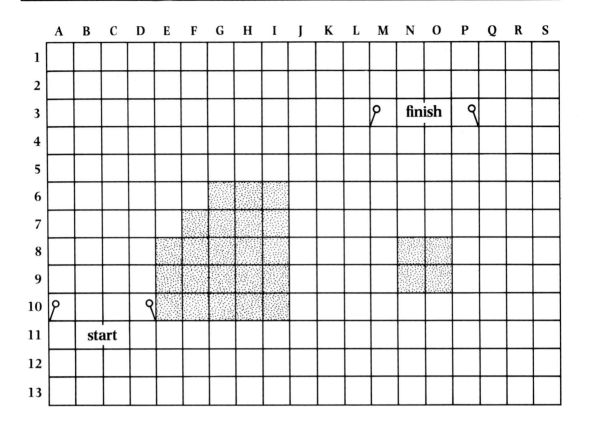

The course that the horses have to go round is shown in the second diagram. You may use as many or as few horses as you wish, but they must all start behind the starting line (in rows 11, 12 or 13), cross the starting line between the posts, go round the main obstacle, circle clockwise round the small obstacle, and cross the finishing line between the posts in the correct direction. All the horses must end up in rows 1, 2 or 3, and must have crossed the finishing line between the posts. (That is, a legal move to cross the finishing line will have either: the horse jumped over being in row 4, and the horse doing the jumping either starting or ending in column M, N, O or P; or, the horse jumped over being in row 3, and the horse doing the jumping starting in column M, N, O or P.)

What is the smallest number of moves you can get round in?

5 Sports and games

SPORTS QUESTIONS

85 Football formations

The manager of the Overnet football team decided to play with an old-fashioned 2–3–5 line-up; i.e. two in defence, three in midfield and five forwards, plus of course a goalkeeper. The players' shirts were each numbered with a different number from 1 to 11. It was noticed that the sums of the numbers on the defence (excluding the goalkeeper), the midfield and the forwards were all the same.

Their opponents Veropolli used a 4–3–3 line-up. Again, their shirts were numbered 1 to 11, and the sum of the numbers on the three forwards was the same as the sum on the three midfield men, but this sum was twice the sum on the defenders' shirts (again, excluding the goalkeeper).

Every defender marked a forward with the same number. Who played where?

86 Golf course

It's a lovely day for a little exercise and sport in picturesque surroundings. So what could be better than a quick nine holes of golf?

The diagrams on the next five pages give maps of nine holes, each divided up into a grid of squares, with numbers on them. The flag is marked with an 'F', and the tee area is shown with bold numbers – you may start from any of the squares on the tee. At each stroke, you must move exactly the number of spaces indicated by the square you are on, in any of the eight directions (N, NE, E, SE, S, SW, W, NW). You may travel over, but not land on, blank 'squares'. Your aim, of course, is to get to the hole in as few strokes as possible.

Hole 1
Par 4

												5	5	5	5	5	5	5	
8	8	7	7	6	6	5	5	5	5	5	4	5	5	2	2	3	3	3	4
7	7	7	7	7	7	7	7	5	5	4	4	5	5	2	1	1	1	4	4
9	7	7	7	7	7	7	6	5	5	4	4	5	5	2	1	F	1	4	4
9	9	7	8	8	6	6	6	5	5	4	5	5	5	2	1	1	1	4	4
9	9	8	8	8	6	6	5	5	5	5	5	5	3	1	1	1	2	4	4
9	8	8	7	7	7	7	7	7	7	5	5	5	3	3	3	2	2	2	
9	8	7	7	7	7	7	7	7	7	7	5	5	5	5	5	5	5		

Hole 2
Par 3

				5	5	4	4	5	5	
	9	9	8	5	5	5	5	4	4	5
9	9	9	8	7	5	4	4	4	3	4	5
9	9	9	7	7	7	3	4	4	3	4	4
9	9	8	7	6	5	3	2	2	2	2	3
9	9	8	7	5	5	3	2	1	2	2	3
6	6	7	7	6	6	2	2	1	F	1	3
8	8	8	7	6	6	3	1	1	1	3	3
7	8	7	7	4	4	3	1	3	3	3	3
6	4	7	7	4	5	4	4	4	4	3	
5	4	5	5	5	5	5	5	4	4	4	

Hole 3
Par 4

2	2	3	3	3	3	3	4	4	4	6	6	6	6	7	7	7	7	8	8	9			
3	2	2	1	1	1	3	4	4	4	1	1	6	6	7	7	7	8	8	8	9	9	9	
3	2	1	1	F	1	1	4	5	5	1	1	6	6	7	7	7	7	8	8	8	9	9	9
3	2	1	1	1	1	2	2	5	5	5	6	6	7	7	7	7	7	8	9	9	9	9	9
3	3	1	4	4	4	3	3	3	5	5	6	6	7	7	7	7	7	8	9	9	8	8	7
	3	4	4	4	4	4	1	1	6	6	6	7	7	7	7	8	8	8	8	8	8	8	7
	3	3	3	3	3	4	1	1	6	6	6	7	7	7	7	7	8	8	8	8	8	8	8
		3	3	3	3	4	4	5											8	8	8	8	8
																				8	8	8	7
																					8	8	7
																					9	**9**	**6**
																					9	**7**	**7**
																					7	**7**	**7**

Hole 4
Par 5

	9	9	9	9	9	9	8	8	8	5	5	4	4	4	4	4	3	3	3	3	3
	9	9	9	9	9	9	9	8	6	5	5	5	5	4	3	3	3	1	1	1	3
4	9	9	9	9	8	8	8	8	6	6	5	5	7	7	3	4	3	1	F	2	4
4	9	9	9	9	8	8	6	6	6	6	6	7	7	4	3	4	3	1	1	2	4
6	8	9	7	7	8	8	8	7	7	7	6	5	5	5	4	4	3	3	3	4	4
6	9	9	7	7	7	7	7	3	3	3	3	3							3	4	4
6	6	7	7	7	6	6	4	4	3	3											
6	6	6	7	7	6	4	4														
	6	6	6	6																	
	6	6	6																		
	6	6	6																		
	9	**8**	**8**																		
	8	**8**	**7**																		
	8	**8**	**7**																		

Hole 5
Par 4

		3	3	3	3	3	3	3	3	3	3	3	3	3	3	3	3	3	3		
	3	3	3	3	9	9	9	9	9	9	9	9	9	9	3	3	3	3	3	3	3	3
3	3	3	9	9	9	9	9	9	9	9	9	9	7	7	7	3	3	3	3	3	3	3	3
3	3	9	9	9	9	9	9	9	9	8	8	9	7	7	7	7	7	3	3	3	3	3	3
9	**9**	**9**	9	9	2	2	2	4	4	8	4	4	4	4	7	7	7	7	5	5	5	2	2
9	**9**	**4**	2	2	2	2	2	2	2	2	4	4	4	4	7	7	7	7	5	5	5	2	2
4	**4**	**4**	2	2	2	2	2	2	2	2	2	4	4	4	4	4	7	7	7	5	5	5	2
2	2	2	2	2	2	2	2	2	2	2	4	4	3	3	3	3	3	7	7	7	5	5	2
	2	2	2	2	2	2	2	2	2	2	3	3	6	3	3	3	3	7	7	1	1	5	2
		4	4	4	4	4	4	8	2	2	2	6	6	1	1	3	3	3	1	1	2	2
			4	4	4	4	8	8	8	2	6	6	1	1	3	3	3	3	2	2	2
				4	4	4	4	4	8	8	6	6	6	2	2	2	2	2	2	2	2
					5	5	4	4	4	6	6	6	6	3	3	3	3	3	3	3	2
					5	5	4	4	6	6	1	1	3	3	1	1	1	3	2
							6	6	1	1	3	2	1	**F**	1	2	2
							6	6	6	3	2	1	1	1	2	2
								6	3	2	2	2	2	2	2

Hole 6
Par 3

			5	5	5	5	5	5	5	5	
		5	5	4	4	4	4	4	4	4	4
		5	5	5	4	5	3	3	1	1	1	3
		5	5	6	4	2	3	2	1	1	2	3
		6	6	6	4	2	3	1	**F**	2	2	3
	8	6	6	6	6	3	3	2	2	1	2	3
	8	8	6	6	6	6	3	3	3	2	2	2	3
	8	8	7	6	6	6	3	3	3	2	2	5	5
6	**8**	**8**	8	7	6	6	3	3	3	3	2	2	5	3
6	**7**	**9**	9	7	7	5	5	3	3	7	7	5	5	3
6	**7**	**9**	9	9	7	6	5	5	5	7	5	7	5	5
		9	9	9	6	6	6	5	5	5	5	5	7

Hole 7
Par 4

1	2	3	4	5	6	7	8	9	10	11	12	13	14	15	16	17	18	19	20	21	22	23
7	**7**	**7**	7	7	9	9	9	9	4	4	4	4	4	4	4							
8	**7**	**7**	7	7	7	9	9	9	7	7	7	4	4	4	4	4	4	4				
8	**7**	**8**	7	7	5	5	5	9	5	7	7	7	5	5	5	4	4	4	4	4		
5	8	8	5	5	5	5	5	5	7	7	7	7	7	7	4	4	4	4	3	3	3	
5	5	5	5	5	5	5	5	7	7	7	7	7	7	4	4	4	3	3	3	2	3	3
5	5	5	5	8	8	7	7	7	7	7	7	7	4	4	4	4	3	1	1	2	3	3
5	9	9	9	8	8	8	8	6	6	6	6	4	4	4	4	5	3	1	1	2	3	3
9	9	9	9	9	9	8	8	8	6	6	6	6	6	5	5	5	3	1	**F**	2	3	3
	9	4	4	4	4	8	8	6	8	6	6	6	6	5	5	5	3	1	1	2	3	
		4	4	4	8	8	8	8	8	8	8	8	5	5	5	3	3	3	3	3		
			8	8	8	8	8	8	8	8	5	5	5	5	5	3	3	3				
					8	8	8	5	5	5	3	3	3	3								

Hole 8
Par 5

1	2	3	4	5	6	7	8	9	10	11	12	13	14	15	16	17
				3	3	3	3	3								
			3	1	1	2	2	2	3							
		5	3	3	3	1	**F**	1	1	3	4					
		5	4	3	3	2	2	1	2	6	4					
	5	4	4	4	3	3	2	2	4	1	3	3				
4	5	5	5	3	3	2	3	2	1	4	2					
4	4	5	3	4	6	3	3	3	3	1	2	3				
4	4	4	5	5	6	6	3	6	1	1	3	3	7			
4	5	5	5	5	5	7	7	1	5	5	3	7	7			
	6	6	6	6	6	7	5	5	7	6	7	5	5			
	6	6	6	7	7	7	7	6	6	5	5	5	5	5		
	6	7	7	7	7	6	6	6	6	6	6	7	7	9		
	6	6	6	6	6	6	6	6	6	6	7	7	9	**9**	**9**	**8**
	6	8	8	8	8	8	8	8	7	7	9	9	9	**9**	**8**	**8**
	5	5	5	7	9	7	7	7	7	7	7	9	9	**9**	**8**	**8**

Hole 9
Par 4

```
9 9 9 9 9 9 9 9 1 1 9 8 8 7 7 6 5
9 9 9 9 9 9 9 1 1 9 8 8 7 6 6 5 5 1 1
9 9 9 9 9 9 9 1 1 9 8 7 6 6 5 5 1 1 2 2 2 2
9 9 9 9 9 9 9 9 1 1 7 7 6 6 5 1 1 4 2 2 2 2 2
9 9 9 9 9 9 9 8 1 1 7 7 6 6 1 1 4 4 4 3 5 5 5 5 2
9 9 9 9 9 9 9 8 8 7 1 6 6 6 5 1 1 4 3 3 3 3 3 3 5
9 9 9 9 9 9 8 8 8 7 1 1 6 5 5 5 1 1 3 3 1 1 1 3 5 2
9 9 9 9 9 9 8 8 7 7 1 1 6 5 5 4 1 1 3 3 1 F 1 3 5 2
9 9 9 9 9 8 8 7 7 7 1 6 6 5 5 4 1 1 3 3 1 1 1 3 5 2
9 9 9 9 8 8 7 7 7 1 1 6 5 5 4 4 4 1 1 3 3 3 3 3 5
9 9 9 9 8 8 7 7 7 1 1 5 5 5 4 4 3 1 1 3 3 5 5 5
9 9 9 8 8 7 7 7 6 6 1 1 5 4 4 4 3 3 1 1
9 9 9 8 8 7 7 6 6 5 1 1 4 4
```

87   A northern league

Hidden in a part of the north there is a very obscure football league with four teams – Grange United, Cartmel Wanderers, Alithwaite Academicals and Lindale Town. At the end of each season, points are awarded to each team, with 4 for first place, 3 for second, 2 for third and 1 for last.

Over a period of twelve seasons, Grange United amassed 32 points, Cartmel Wanderers 31, Alithwaite Academicals 30 and Lindale Town 27. During this period, Grange United consistently ended two, but never more than two, seasons in the same position, and overall they occupied each position at least twice. Cartmel Wanderers never finished in the same position two years running, and Alithwaite Academicals never achieved three consecutive years in the same position. Lindale Town, on the other hand, always finished in the same position for three consecutive seasons, and they were never champions.

The league positions at the end of the third and twelfth seasons were identical, and so too were the placings at the end of the second and tenth seasons. In the fifth season Alithwaite Academicals retained the championship, and Grange United improved one position to become runners-up.

What were the placings at the end of the ninth season?

88 Three-dart finishes
(a) What is the highest three-dart finish in which the third dart's score exceeds that of the second, which exceeds that of the first?
(b) What is the third highest prime number from which there is a three-dart finish?
(c) What is the highest score from which there are precisely three essentially different three-dart finishes?

89 Tennis match
At the end of a gruelling five-set match of tennis between Smith and Jones (in which tie-breaks were to be used to decide the first four sets if the score reached six all), both players had won 33 games. In the first set, which Smith won, half as many games were played as in the second set. There were also half as many games played in the fourth set as in the fifth. Who won the match, and what were the scores in each set?

90 World Cup
For the second round in the recent football World Cup finals, teams that finished first or second in their groups went forward automatically, together with the best four of the six third placed. On the draw for the second round these four places were designated as:

Venue 1: Third in group A, B or D;
Venue 2: Third in group C, E or F;
Venue 3: Third in group A, B or F;
Venue 4: Third in group C, D or E.

There was then some leeway in who played where. When, for instance, B, D, E and F were the best four, they could have gone to the venues in the order B, E, F, D or D, F, B, E. The designation of the four places in fact gave two choices whichever four were to go through, except that if it had been A, B, C and E then there would have been four choices!

Somehow the organizers managed with their choice to hit upon the one which gave the greatest leeway overall, totalled over all possibilities for the four teams that could go through. Still, it could have been worse. They obviously had to make sure that, whichever four went through, a venue could be assigned to each according to the prescription; but they might have specified the second round draw in a way that would have allowed five choices if A, B, C and E had qualified. Can you find such a second round draw?

91   The big race

The big race of the day featured just seven runners: Aldini, Burnt Oak, Curl, Desert Rose, Escarmouche, Fountain and Gregale. Olive was there with six friends, and they each decided to back a different horse.

Ken's horse trailed in a bad last place. Numbers 1 and 2 finished in fourth and fifth places, though not necessarily in that order. No horse finished in a position that was the same as its number. Number 1 was either Aldini or Curl.

The race was won by number 4, Desert Rose, which just beat Ian's horse. Mandy's fancy, Gregale, was not in the first four, but horse number 3 was. Escarmouche was second.

Leslie's choice, which was not Burnt Oak nor Curl, finished fifth. John's horse, Aldini, finished behind number 6. Nigel's horse was Burnt Oak or Fountain.

What was the number of each of the horses, in which position did they finish, and who backed what?

92   A frame of snooker

Potter and Plant played a frame of snooker, neither of them giving away penalty points; subject to that, the total number of points was as high as it could have been. Potter potted more blacks, but although he pocketed the last ball he still potted fewer balls overall. Who won, and which balls were potted by whom?

GAMES

93   Football manager

Each player is the manager of a football team with limited funds at his disposal. The team he fields for a season is determined by eleven whole numbers (zero or above) that sum to 100. The competition runs for five seasons. At the end of that time the total points each team achieves will decide the winner (followed by goal difference, followed by goals scored). Points for each match are 3 for a win, 1 for a draw, 0 for a loss.

The outcome of each match is determined by comparing the two sets of numbers. For each of a player's numbers that is more than 2 above his opponent's corresponding number, he is credited with a goal.

So if A had: 8,   2, 10, 10,   7, 12, 19, 10,   8, 11,   3
and B had: 11,   4, 25,   9,   8,   7,   9, 12, 10,   3,   2
then the goals
would be: B   –   B   –   –   A   A   –   –   A   –

i.e. A wins by 3 goals to 2.

Once everyone has chosen for the season, all the line-ups are made public, and the scores are calculated. Players may then change their line-up (completely, a bit or not at all) for the next season, and the process repeats.

That's the way the game is played with a number of players. If you want to treat it as a puzzle, though, then see how well you would have done when this puzzle was first proposed. Write down your choice of numbers, and play them against the four team formations shown in the hints. Would you have won?

94   Tictactics

Two players indulge in the following game. In an ordinary noughts and crosses grid, 3×3, they alternately mark Xs and Os until each has marked four; the last square is left blank. Then the X player secretly selects a row, and the O player secretly selects a column. Both players then reveal their selections, and the symbol in the selected row and column is examined. If it is blank then the game is a draw, but otherwise the player whose symbol it is wins that round. This secret selection is then repeated, say five times in all, and the overall game is then repeated as necessary.

95   The threepenny game

The threepenny game is played as follows. Using a penny and a twopenny piece, you and your opponent take turns with the aim of achieving a total of at least ten pence in heads. If you do this before your opponent can, you receive the prize money from her; if you lose, you must pay the prize money to her.

Initially the prize money is one penny. On each turn, a player may elect either to throw or to raise the prize by one penny. If she chooses to throw, she tosses the two coins and adds the value of the heads to her total (i.e. 3 if both are heads, 2 if just the twopence is, 1 if just the penny is, 0 if neither is heads). The turn then passes to her opponent. If, though, she chooses to raise the prize, the turn passes immediately to her opponent; but the prize money cannot be raised above ten pence.

Of course, chance comes into this a lot, but then so does the tactics of knowing when to toss the coins and when to raise the prize money. In actual play, about twenty games should even out the luck, and the player with the better strategy should be ahead.

96   Football director

You are a director of three football clubs. Of course, you're not allowed to have two in the same division, and you have one in the first, one in the second and one in the third.

With your considerable financial resources, you are able to buy players to strengthen various areas of each of your teams. In fact, the strength of any team is described by three positive whole numbers: one for attack (1–10), one for midfield (1–10) and one for defence (1–10). Your financial assets limit the total strengths for the three zones of your three teams to 40.

All you have to do is choose three triplets of numbers, the nine numbers totalling 40, so that your teams will be the most successful. Success will be measured in terms of league position at the end of the season. To find out league position, every team in each division will play every other team twice, with 2 points awarded for a win, 1 for a draw and 0 for a loss.

The score in each match is determined by the strengths of the two teams meeting. The number of good attacks a side has is determined by its midfield domination, and the proportion of good attacks that end in goals is determined by the attack's domination over the defence.

Specifically, if a team with attack/midfield/defence strengths of $a/b/c$ meets one of strengths $d/e/f$, then the game proceeds as follows. Think of there being three regions of the pitch: the second team's attack, the midfield, and the first team's attack. The ball starts in midfield, and on each turn after that the ball moves in the first team's favour with a probability depending on the two opposing strengths. That is, from the second team's attack to midfield the chance is $c/(c+d)$; from there to the first team's attack the chance is $b/(b+e)$; and from there to scoring a goal the chance is $a/(a+f)$. The chances for the ball moving in the second team's favour are calculated in a corresponding way.

Whenever a goal is scored, the ball returns to midfield for the kick-off. Full time is after twenty turns.

Your teams must be assigned to the first, second and third divisions according to their total strength (i.e. $a+b+c$ or $d+e+f$ in the example above), so that the strength of your first division team is no less than that of your second, which is no less than that of your third.

If you can find enough people to play this with (at least three would be best), then you can simply play the game. If, instead, you want to see how well you would have done when the problem was first set, first work out how your teams will enter, and then look at the example in the hints.

Work out the scores in all the matches as described, and then assign league positions in the normal way. Finally, the director of the bottom team in Division 1 gets 5 points, the second bottom 10 points, then 15, etc. according to the number of players. For Division 2 the point assignment is 4, 8, 12, . . . going upwards, and for Division 3 it is 3, 6, 9, . . .

The overall winner is the director with the highest score. Good luck!

97   Greetings

Nearly everyone plays a game very similar to 'Greetings' without realizing it. You see, it's enjoyable to receive Christmas cards from people, but it can be a bit of a chore to buy, write and send them oneself. It's probably three times as interesting to receive a card as to send one.

'Greetings' involves a number of players, and one 'postman'. If possible, the postman's role can be taken by a computer, leaving everyone free to play. The game takes place over a fixed number of rounds, or 'years' – say, fifteen.

Each year everyone sends a card to as many or as few of the others as he or she wishes, and this is done by everyone simultaneously, and secretly. This is effected by each player indicating to the 'postman' what his or her play is, and the 'postman' then informing each player whom he has received cards from. The 'postman' should, however, randomly fail to deliver a predetermined proportion of cards (say one in ten). (If desired, this refinement can be omitted.)

The players do not know how many cards the other players have received each year. In standard play, the participants should be referred to in some coded way, so that no-one knows the actual identity of the person who sent him or her a card, although he or she will notice (say) that the same person sent a card the previous year. (As an option, this anonymity can be dropped, and the real names of the players can be used.)

At the end of the predetermined number of rounds, each player's score is calculated as three times the number of cards he or she received, minus the number of cards he or she sent. The winner is then the player with the highest score.

98   Clamber

The game of 'clamber' can be played on a square board of any size (except the very small), and with different numbers of pieces. The main form, however, is played on the familiar 8×8 board, with five pieces each, starting as shown in the diagram.

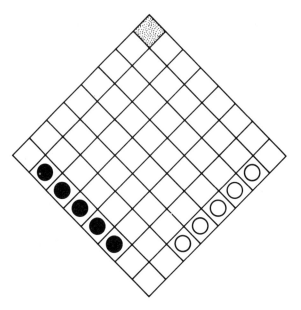

One particular corner of the board represents the 'top', and the object of the game is to get one of your pieces to the top first. Pieces move like chess knights. If your move lands on one of your opponent's pieces, instead of it being captured, it slides three squares orthogonally downwards (in either downwards direction, at your opponent's discretion). If any of these three squares is occupied by either player's piece, they too slide three squares orthogonally downwards (in the direction of the owner's choice). If a complex 'avalanche' starts, the order in which the slides are made may be important: in this case, as soon as one piece's square is occupied (at the end of a move or during a slide), its slide is attended to before returning to that of the piece that caused its slide. If a piece would be taken outside the confines of the board by a slide, the board must be thought of as being extended. Players alternate in moving, choosing whichever of their pieces they wish.

Instead of the standard form of the game, other initial arrangements of pieces and sizes of boards can be tried. It is interesting to work out the one-piece-per-side game, where the two pieces start symmetrically; find out which starting positions give the first player a win, and which give the second player a win.

99   One-day cricket

You are the captain of your cricket team in a one-day single-innings competition. Each innings is limited to a maximum of 200 balls, and of course a maximum of ten wickets to fall. If the scores finish level, the result is a tie, irrespective of how many wickets each side has lost.

Your bowlers and fielders can be relied upon to do their utmost for you, so there's really only one area where you can decide the team's tactics. That is, by instructing your batsmen when to play safely and when to take risks. Statisticians have established that when a batsman plays safely his probability of scoring a run off a ball is 0.4, and his probability of being out is 0.02. (Only one run per ball can be scored in this simplified game, and it is impossible to score and be out off the same ball.) When a batsman is taking risks, the probability of a run is 0.8 and the probability of being out is 0.1.

This can be played with a calculator or a computer to give you random numbers. Then you can decide, ball by ball, on whether to play safely or riskily. Alternatively, you could decide on tactics beforehand, and then program a computer to play through the whole game for you. The randomness within one game will affect the result greatly, but over a total of ten games batting first and ten games batting second against someone, the luck will probably have evened out, and the player with the better tactics should be the overall winner.

100   Dodgem

The game of 'dodgem' involves two players, and a square board of any size from 3×3 upwards. This smallest board already gives an interesting game.

The two players each start with the same number of pieces, one fewer than the side of the square. Label the four orthogonal directions N, E, S, W in the obvious way. Then the square in the SW corner starts unoccupied, black starts with his pieces filling the remaining squares on the S side of the board, and white starts with her pieces on the W side, as shown in the diagram.

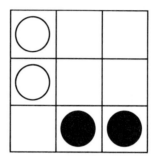

At each turn, a player may move any one of his or her pieces that is on the board; black may only move one square at a time N, E or W, and white may only move one square at a time E, S or N. A piece may be moved off the board, but only in the N direction for black, and the E direction for white. The aim of the game is to be the first player to move all your pieces off the board. If, though, you 'stalemate' your opponent by leaving him or her without a legal move, then you lose instantly.

Obviously, you want to limit the number of sideways moves (i.e. E or W for black, and N or S for white) that you make; these get you no nearer the destination. However, such a sideways move can often obstruct your opponent, and cause him or her to make more than one sideways move.

6 Hints

The puzzles in this book are designed to entertain, but even if questions have defeated you at first look, a few suggestions as to methods of attack may help you to solve them.

The numbering within this chapter follows that in the individual chapters. Chapter headings are repeated, but not the titles of individual puzzles.

STARTERS

1 It involves the words for the numbers.

2 This can be done with six words apart from the two given.

3 A number and its position in the series gives the next number.

4 A straight substitution cipher, although the coding of letters to numbers has a slight twist.

5 Some of the letters, taken together, might throw some light on the series.

6 If you're not using a dictionary, you can consider you've got one of the shortest solutions if you have four intermediate words. There is, though, a shorter solution using a word (of Dutch origin, though accepted in English as well) for Afrikaans.

7 How many numbers are there in the series? Does that suggest what items might be represented? Now can you think of a way of coding them as numbers?

8 If you want to score highly, it's probably better to go for a lot of shortish (four- or five-letter) words, rather than trying to find longer ones.

9 A calculator might help you solve this one.

10 This involves the digits that make up each number.

11 This can be done with four intermediates, and the key word is a rarely used word for 'fragments'.

12   There are the same number of elements in this sequence as there were for the one in puzzle no. 7.

13   Work methodically through; *e* and *c* should be immediate, but then the choices for *a* and *g* are limited, and so on.

14   This isn't a sequence, rather a set of letters with some property.

15   This needs six intermediate words.

16   A little bit of investigation of the 22 three-digit squares will get you there.

17   Each number is the first of a certain sort.

18   This needs six intermediate words.

THE ADVENTURES OF THE SEVEN DWARFS

19   The amounts by which the letters change (Q to S, U to W, etc.) are 2, 2, 3, 4, 6. What is the next number in that sequence?

20   Just keep trying!

21   The heights are purely nominal.

22   The suit held by only three people must be an eleven-card one, split 4–4–3, but it can't be clubs because Grumpy holds those. Grumpy's holding is also important when you consider what spades Dozey or Jock could have. Then determine how many spades are left and who could have them.

23   Recall that the dwarfs came up with numbers 'after lengthy consideration'.

24   To finish opposite their rooms, Grumpy must have been in Bossy's or Doc's, and Dopey must have been in Hairy's or Jock's; but Grumpy and Dopey ended up next to each other, so you know where they were. In a similar way you can find where Bossy and Doc finished. If you then consider the arrangements for the other three dwarfs, you will find that only one arrangement fits all the conditions.

25   Assume, in turn, it was each of the dwarfs. Then see if the conditions can hold. If Bossy's audible statement is true, then his muttered one will have been identical; but if his audible statement is false, he may have muttered a different false statement.

26   A straightforward matter of trying all the possibilities.

27   If the original height of the bar was h units, then the width was $2h$ units and the length was $4h$ units; therefore the volume was $8h^3$ cubed units. If the new height is k units, then each of the chunks is $4k \times 4k \times k$ units. With the new shape, if n of the chunks fit across the width, then $2n$ fit along the length. The new volume of

the whole bar then comes out at $8nk \times 4nk \times k = 32n^2k^3$ cubed units; however, this equals the original $8h^3$. If the slab had been in the cupboard for t hours, then the steady dwindling of the height means that $k = [(120-t)/120] \times h$. Now you must find whole numbers for t and n that fit the equations.

28   There are two separate little 'episodes' played out with the basket. In each of these there are three essentially different starting apples: middle of one of the sides, one of the corners, or one of the six in the inner ring (the central apple can't be the starting one, because then the rotation would have no effect). The little old lady moves the basket whenever Snow White is about to select an unpoisoned apple, but does nothing if the apple is a poisoned one. For each of these starting apples, you can work out the sequence of poisoned and unpoisoned apples. Occasionally there are two choices for how a move might have gone, but one or other option becomes impossible later. Then it is a matter of fitting together one arrangement from the first 'episode' with one from the second, suitably rotated to fit together to agree on the poisoned and unpoisoned apples.

29   This three-dimensional trigonometry problem can be rapidly transformed into a two-dimensional one, if you let the height of the tower be x and then calculate the distances of the three dwarfs from the base.

30   Concentrate first on the seven dwarfs, and find out which day's trap each one discovered. The traps themselves and the times at which they were discovered will then fall into place with just a few gaps. These gaps can then be filled by considering the possible times, remembering that all the times are different.

31   The conditions of the question tell you that the size of the army can be expressed as either x^2 or $7y^2 + 1$ (x is the side of the united square, and y the side of each general's square). The 'bit of subtlety and then some brute force' suggested in the question is as follows. You can rewrite the equation as $x^2 - 1 = 7y^2$, to be solved in whole numbers, $x^2 - 1 = (x+1)(x-1)$; and so 7 must divide either $x+1$ or $x-1$. The limits given for the size of the whole square mean that x lies between 100 and 316. More analysis could take you further, but now's the best time for some brute force!

32   Nothing for this but to keep trying. The number you are trying to reach is y, the side of the small squares, in the previous question. If you haven't yet solved that question, you may be interested to know that, if Snow White had had to do the same, she could have come up with $S + N - O + W + W + H - I - T + E$.

33   Careful trial and error, and suitable readjustment of combinations that are nearly right, should get you there, if you keep at it.

34   The speeds shouldn't be too difficult to find, and then it's a matter of a bit of Pythagoras and some simple sums.

35   The best way to start this is to look at the possible relative positions of G, F and A.

G to F must be at least two more than F to A (because C to D is intermediate in length), and G to A must be at most six. Then all that is left is to fit E, C and D in, and B takes the space that is left.

36   You know that some of the numbers occur only once, so work out the possibilities bearing in mind that the other numbers may or may not be repeated. Then recheck them, remembering that the prince applied the same degree of turn at the same type of junction.

37   Go through all the statements methodically; list all the gifts, and then assign the fantasies and names to them when you can. Hairy and Grumpy can be placed rapidly, so too can Bossy, and then Jock is the only one who can go with a particular gift. Then, studying the fantasies should give you enough information to solve the problem completely.

38   This is a very complicated problem, but it can be solved in a number of shortish steps, each of which clears up some unknowns and leaves only a few possibilities for some others. The starting point is that Dopey did actually have some tea; but don't assume that Hairy necessarily had some. Later on, Grumpy contradicts Jock, so one must be telling the truth and the other lying. Deductions can be made from this, and then assume that Hairy is or is not lying; count up the tea drinkers, examine Dopey's number-of-liars statement, and one way will give a contradiction while the other leads nearer the solution. Now you can start on the dwarfs' other names. Get as far as you can with certainty, then make assumptions but be prepared to backtrack if you find a contradiction.

THE ISLE OF MARANGA

39   There's really nothing for this but trial and error! You may find it helpful to write the three weather cycles on strips of paper, which you can then slide about until they match in a way that fits the conditions.

40   Straightforward algebra will get you there; just try not to make mistakes!

41   Let the required measurements be x, y and z chisen, and set up equations for the areas. You will get two independent equations in three unknowns, but because they must be solved in integers you will find that there is only one solution.

42   Between 1901 and 2099 the calendar repeats every 28 years. The most straightforward thing to do is to work out the day of the week that 1 January fell on in each of the last 28 years, and then find when (if at all) St Tarnop's day occurred each year.

43   By considering the four meanings of the lights, you can work out what combinations you could have without encouraging accidents. There is then only one way that the colours shown can be assigned to the different meanings, and from that you can discover which of the cars can proceed.

44   This is a variation of puzzle no. 71, and it would probably help if you attempted that one first. On the one hand, you have less information here, because some of the names on the signposts are missing. On the other hand, you have the added information that you can map out the villages and interconnecting roads with no roads crossing. A good starting point is Blimpscoe: no signpost has room for more than four names on it; it cannot be the site of either signpost with room for four names, because it is named on the only two of these; it cannot have fewer than three neighbours, because it is already named on three signposts; therefore it must have exactly three neighbours. If you try various possibilities for which numbered signpost goes with which village, and what the missing names are, you will find all the possibilities except one ruled out by the fact that you can draw the map.

45   The appearances of the windows depend on the remainders left when the room numbers are divided by 5 (for shape), 4 (for drape), 7 (for colour) and 12 (for glazing), but the glazing arrangement introduces a complication.

46   The clues as to the lengths of the notes give only very few possible arrangements. Then the fact that A is not rung within the first six beats limits things further. After that, judicious trial and error will get you there.

47   This needs experimentation. A few diagrams might help you, but it's probably best to make some shapes and keep trying.

48   For some of the fifteen slabs there is only one possible position in the pattern; try to find these and then fit the others around them.

49   This is tricky, and there probably is no methodical approach. As a clue, though, the two shapes are mirror images of each other.

50   To make the explanations easier, let us assume that the castle is aligned with the compass, so that there are north-, south-, east- and west-facing walls. A little

thought and experimentation with small examples will reveal two useful facts for any such problem. First, the number of north- and south-facing walls together equals the number of east- and west-facing walls (because they alternate round the perimeter). Second, the total length of all the north-facing walls equals the total of the south-facing ones, and similarly the east-facing total equals the west-facing total. These observations should enable you to find which lengths of wall could face in which directions. It is then a matter of arranging them to enclose the stated area, making sure than no two walls ever cross each other.

51   When you multiply 7 precops by 100, you get a whole number of versils plus 18 precops; this limits the number of precops in a versil to only a few choices. Then studying the arpep and versil will eliminate all but one of the possibilities.

52   This can be attacked algebraically, or by enumerating all the ways that the stated situations could have occurred. As a start, though, you can quickly see that without loss of generality you want $2x+y+z=28$, and either $x+2y+2z=21$ or $x+3y+z=21$. (Since 28 is more than 21, you can't have 2 xs or more in the second sum.)

53   A little algebra followed by some trial and error is needed here. Say there are n mathofs in a grunolf, and the estate is x grunolfs y mathofs on each side, and the area is z square grunolfs and 1770 square mathofs. Then $(xn+y)^2=zn^2+1770$. Now $(xn+y)^2=x^2n^2+2xyn+y^2$, so you have to find out how many whole square grunolfs there are in this. If $2xy=pn+q$ (where $q<n$) then you can look at square grunolfs and square mathofs separately. Either $x^2+p=z$ and $y^2+qn=1770$, or there is a carry so that $x^2+p+1=z$ and $y^2+qn-n^2=1770$. The simplest starting point is to try various values of y, and solve $qn=1770-y^2$ or $n(n-q)=y^2-1770$ in the two cases; the question gives limits for n^2 and z.

54   Just proceed carefully, and you'll get there!

55   This is a little fiddly, but the easiest method to explain is as follows. You know, for instance, that a,b,e is not a magical set, but that if any other item is added then it will be a magical set. So, if c is added, you can conclude that one of b,c,e or a,c,e or a,b,c is a mystical set, or failing that, a,b,c,e is. By eliminating from these the sets you know are not mystical, you can progress with the solution.

56   You need to solve the previous question (or at least look up the answer!) before attempting this one. Once you know what the magical sets are, you can investigate the various plays in the little game that St Tarnop and Hastaman engage in.

57   With a little algebra for the fight sequence you will find that the original area is a certain multiple of the size of the final piece. A search through the sums of consecutive prime numbers, for numbers with this certain factor, should then lead you to the solution.

58 You could work out the equation for the sum of all numbers from m to n, and then try solutions for a total of 680–689, bearing in mind that you want m in the range 20–29 and n in the range 40–49. Alternatively, you could guess a starting and finishing age, work out the sum, and then adjust it suitably at either end until a sum of 680–689 is reached.

59 There are six arrangements for the courts A, B and C to meet at intervals of three, five and eight years. The overall pattern for these meetings will repeat after the lowest common multiple (LCM) of three, five and eight years, i.e. 120 years, which is obviously longer than Olnic could reign. The most straightforward method of solution is to try the six arrangements, and to see which could have given the stated conditions, and thus how long he must have reigned.

60 This could be solved algebraically, but the complications of the leap year (every year divisible by 4 except 1700) mean that the simplest method of solution is probably just trial and error.

61 This is fairly simple to state, but the solution takes a bit of finding. What you have to do is divide the whole numbers between 1703 and 1845 inclusive into five sets of consecutive numbers; each of the sets must be labelled E, B or S (for the three houses), such that if you add 102 to years in a set labelled E, subtract 9 from those labelled B, and subtract 60 from those labelled S, you still have each of the years from 1703 to 1845 occurring once. To solve the problem you need to set up all the possible arrangements of the E, B and S houses, in both our and their dating system, so that there are five letters but with adjacent letters being different. Then you can derive equations for the lengths of rule of the houses, until you find one that the stated numbers satisfy.

62 The lengths of rule only come in at the end of the solution, once you have discovered the order of the reigns, so ignore them to begin with. If you work out which kings can be followed by which, you should then discover that there are only a few arrangements of all nine, and all but one of these will be ruled out by the fact that two brothers can't have the same name.

63 Knowing the notes of the chord D7, you can work out the possible notes of each open string. Then do the same thing for the G6 chord, which will further restrict the options. Finally, knowing that the chords contain each note exactly once will lead you to the unique solution.

64 The best way to attack this is probably to try each of the seven notes that could be the lowest, and then see if you can find suitable values for the valves (each raising the pitch by a number of semitones, such that adding them together in appropriate combinations will give all the required notes).

65 If two dampers combine to let through a set of notes, then obviously all of those notes are let through by both dampers; and if you know that two dampers together cut out a particular note, then obviously one or both must individually

cut it out. Considering these two simple principles for chords in the right order, you can deduce which notes are damped and which undamped by each damper.

66   This is really just a case of trying out the various combinations for the C major or D minor chords, and seeing if you can find arrangements that fit together. Bear in mind that in the basic pattern you may not necessarily have an octave of twelve consecutive notes; the rules can still be followed without that happening.

THE MARTIAN DATING AGENCY AND OTHER PROBLEMS

67   It happens that there is only one compatible triple involving Eck, so that's the starting point. Next, you will find that there is only one male compatible with Sed, and only one male compatible with Vod. From there, trial and error shouldn't be too hard.

68   With a little thought, you can see that the sex of a child is the sex of the dominant parent at conception. Now, the same parent can't have had the dominant effect on both Dor and El, or otherwise all their features would be identical. Also, a little mathematics shows that, if one dominant parent was female and the other was numale, then the sum of the genetic scores for Dor and El minus twice that for Ak must be divisible by 3 for all features; but it isn't. So one of Dor and El is male and the other isn't; this gives four possibilities, and you will find that only one of them works when you try to discover the parents' features.

69   From the 'framework' rules you should be able to draw the six allowable positions. There are two positions with the numale's feet in a straight line, three with its left foot and right foot enclosing an angle of $120°$ about its middle foot as it looks forward, and one with its left and right feet enclosing an angle of $240°$. You can then find how the various steps can take you from one position to another, ignoring rotations and translations. From a study of this, and some checking of the combinations of steps, you should then be able to work out how the dance can go.

70   This just needs a methodical approach. For instance, what if one team were the four with pink fur, or four of the five with violet fur? Can you then divide the other eight up in a suitable way? If this fails, try some of the other features, and so on.

71   The basis for solving this is a bit of counting. For instance, Miss Nicholas has four friends within the group; so which of the first names occur four times (because she must be one of them)? This should start you off, and then you can either use trial and error, or pursue the line of finding (say) which girl has four friends, two of whom have three friends and two of whom have five friends.

72   Work out the possibilities for Kevin and Henry, and for Frances and Irene, from the conditions relating to them. Then try fitting the other conditions in. It's better to write down the quantities from one to eleven, and to see which people could have consumed them, than to start with the people and work out the quantities.

73   Trial and error will eventually get you there, but can be very laborious. One very useful observation, though, is that if two charts have at least three records in common, then at least one of the records must be on a genuine 'chart run' of consecutive weeks (because only two records can be 'irregular'). This does not necessarily mean that the two weeks must be consecutive, but they should be very close. If you find all the pairs of weeks that have three or more records in common, you will have only a few possible sequences to check.

74   A little bit of algebra, then possibly some trial and error to solve it in integers, bearing in mind that the gateau is longer than it is high.

75   A little algebra should help in this one. (Let her parents' ages be x and y when she was born, and let her age when I met her be d.) Alternatively, factorizing recent dates might get you to the answer.

76   The numbers can be found directly by algebra; obviously the calculator evaluates any divisions before additions.

77   Nine of the letters appear either at the beginning or at the end of an expression, so the other four must be the signs. Then a quick look at equations 1, 4 and 2 should tell you what three of the signs represent. After that, examining the equations in the right order will quickly give you the solution.

78   (a) Think big! (b) Trial and error!

79   A methodical system of trial and error is needed for this, to be sure that you go through all the possibilities. For instance, you could look at all the ways to place the all-light and all-dark squares, and then fit the others in.

80   You need to experiment a lot in this one, remembering always to leave a way back to the starting square. It's probably a good idea to try to use the lower-numbered squares first, before they become unavailable.

81   There are no short-cuts for the map! Work out all the distances, and then see which fit the clues.

82   This needs trial, error and luck to find the best solution. The best approach is probably to divide the bricks up into ten groups, each totalling twenty units; then arrange these course by course in a sensible way; then see if any of the rows can be slid a bit to get a better solution. Next you could rearrange the courses and repeat some of the process; or you could swop a few bricks around to try to improve things. When you've done all that, start the whole process again!

83   Solving the maze, using the shortest path, is just a matter of time. Decoding the numbers is then not difficult, if you guess what the entrance and exit words are.

84   To find the smallest number of moves, it's best to discover the minimum number of horses that you need. Consider a horse starting on one particular square, and work out all the squares it could possibly visit, if other horses were suitably arranged. Although chess knights can reach any square, the restriction here to clockwise moves only does limit the possible squares. Once you have the minimum number, a little experimentation should get you quite close to the smallest number of moves for the whole course, and the odd refinement may cut the number down still further.

SPORTS AND GAMES

85   Because the defence, midfield and forward totals for Overnet are all the same, the overall total for the outfielders must be a multiple of 3. This then constrains the goalkeeper's number, which is a good starting point. A similar sort of approach will start you off for Veropolli, too. Then comparing the possibilities for the two teams will lead to the answer.

86   It's a good idea to work a stroke or two back from the flag in various ways, and then see how easily you can reach those squares from the tee.

87   You are told where Grange and Alithwaite finished in seasons 4 and 5. From the totals of Grange and Lindale, and the fact that their placings are repetitive, you can work out the number of times they finished in each position. The best way of working towards the solution is to draw up a table of teams and seasons, and write in the number of points each team scored each time. With the similarity of seasons 3 and 12, and 2 and 10, you can complete Grange United's history, and then Lindale Town's. Then complete the placings in the fourth and fifth seasons, and work backwards and forwards from these.

88   If you need a reminder of the scoring, any dart can score from 1 to 20 without bonus, or doubled, or trebled, or can score 25, or 25 doubled. To finish, the last dart of the three must be a double. As to finding the solution, trial and error is all there is for this; if you have a suspicion about (c), you may be right!

89   Note that a set of tennis is won as soon as one player has won at least six games and has at least a two-game lead, unless a tie-break game is used; a tie-break decides the set in favour of the winner but is recorded as simply one more game.

      The number of games in any of the first four sets is quite restricted, and you should rapidly deduce the scores in the first two sets with the information given, although the winner in the second set will not yet be clear. Then you can discover groupings of possible numbers of games in sets three to five, knowing there were twice as many in the fifth as in the fourth. Finally, you have to try to fit the various possibilities together, to find an arrangement that gives the same total of games won by the two players.

90 The solution is not easy to arrive at methodically, so it may just need trial and error.

91 Picking up the information in the right order is the important thing here. You have some definitive information on who came first, second, fifth and seventh, so start with that. Then the fact that 1 and 2 finished fourth and fifth, and that 1 is horse A or C, but that the fifth horse is neither B nor C, should get you further, since you know that A is J's horse and not L's. That much should give you a good foundation for completing the problem.

92 For those who don't know the scoring system, here are the relevant parts. Read them carefully! There are fifteen reds worth 1 point each, and six 'colours', yellow, green, brown, blue, pink and black, worth 2, 3, 4, 5, 6 and 7 points, respectively. When a red is potted, it stays down, but then you have the opportunity of potting a colour of your choice, which is replaced on the table if you succeed. Once all the reds (and the last 'bonus' colour, if applicable) have been potted, the six colours are pocketed in ascending order of value, and they are not replaced. If scores are level at the end of all of this, the black is put back on the table for a deciding 7 points.

93 When this was tried with four players, who shall be labelled United, Wanderers, Rovers and City, the following numbers were chosen.

Season 1

United	8	8	12	12	7	12	13	6	7	10	5
Wanderers	8	8	8	20	8	8	8	8	8	8	8
Rovers	12	12	12	8	8	8	8	8	8	8	8
City	15	16	16	16	16	16	1	1	1	1	1

Season 2

United	4	10	8	9	14	8	8	8	14	8	9
Wanderers	0	15	15	15	15	15	0	15	0	10	0
Rovers	17	0	0	17	17	0	17	0	17	0	15
City	1	15	16	1	16	16	1	16	1	1	16

Season 3

United	17	17	17	0	15	0	17	0	0	17	0
Wanderers	14	14	14	14	14	14	0	0	0	16	0
Rovers	4	18	0	18	17	17	18	0	4	4	0
City	10	15	15	0	0	15	0	15	15	15	0

Season 4

United	15	16	16	0	15	0	16	3	0	16	3
Wanderers	15	0	15	0	20	0	20	0	15	0	15
Rovers	0	17	5	17	17	17	17	5	5	0	0
City	15	15	15	15	15	0	0	25	0	0	0

Season 5

United	15	16	16	0	15	0	16	3	0	16	3
Wanderers	15	0	15	0	20	0	20	15	0	15	0
Rovers	5	5	5	17	17	17	17	17	0	0	0
City	0	17	18	7	8	3	0	20	9	9	9

This meant that Wanderers won with 30 points, then City with 22, United with 19 and Rovers with 13. This did owe a little to random fluctuations; if you replay the above many times, and shuffle the order of the numbers each time, the positions on average will be City, United, Wanderers, Rovers. The best teams for the five seasons on average work out as: City; Wanderers; United; Wanderers; United and City about level.

94   An example game is shown in the diagrams. X plays first, then O, to occupy the spaces in the order shown.

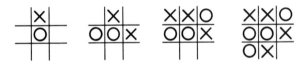

The two players then secretly and simultaneously select the rows and columns indicated, to complete five games with this arrangement.

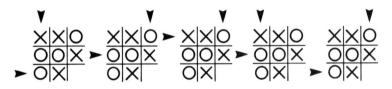

The winners of the five games are thus O, X, O, O, neither. The overall winner of this short match is therefore O, by a score of 3–1.

95   Here is an example. Player A decides to raise the prize whenever she is at least 3 ahead, but B is never prepared to increase it. Six games are played, with A starting in the odd-numbered ones and B in the even-numbered ones. The progress of each game is shown column by column, with new entries showing for A when she throws, for B when she throws, and for 'prize' when the value is increased.

A   0 0   3   4   5
B   0 3   5   8   11
prize 1   Match score A:0 B:1

A   0 3   4   6   8   8
B   0 3   5   6   7   7   10
prize 1   Match score A:0 B:2

A   0 0   2   2   3   5   6 8
B   0 2   3   5   6   6   8   10
prize 1   Match score A:0 B:3

A   0 2   2   3   5   8   11
B   0 0   1   2   2   4   4 6
prize 1   2
                                                     Match score A:2 B:3

A   0 3   6   9   10
B   0 3   3   6   8
prize 1   2   Match score A:4 B:3

A   0   0   1   4   5   6   8   9   12
B   0 3   3   6   6   6   7   7   9
prize 1   Match score A:5 B:3

B had very slightly the worse of the throws, but A made better use of her luck, increasing the prize when she was well ahead, and scored more heavily on the games she won.

96 Here is an example competition with four players, whom we shall label R, C, A and S. The numbers are:

Division		Player R				Player A		
		a	m	d		a	m	d
1	Rangers	6	7	6	Athletic	4	8	4
2	Real	6	6	6	Albion	4	7	3
3	Rovers	1	1	1	Academicals	3	5	2

Division		Player C				Player S		
		a	m	d		a	m	d
1	Celtic	9	6	5	Sporting Club	9	9	4
2	City	5	6	3	Spartans	2	4	4
3	Casuals	1	3	2	Strollers	3	4	1

The results were:

Division 1	Away team				Goals			
	R	A	C	S	F	A	Pts	Posn
Rangers		4–2	3–4	3–3	21	15	8	2nd
Athletic	0–4		4–3	1–6	10	23	3	4th
Celtic	3–3	3–0		2–5	15	20	5	3rd
Sporting Club	3–4	3–3	5–0		25	13	8	1st

Division 2	Away team				Goals			
	R	A	C	S	F	A	Pts	Posn
Real		4–2	5–3	4–0	22	13	10	2nd
Albion	2–1		4–1	2–1	21	8	10	1st
City	3–4	0–5		3–2	14	21	4	3rd
Spartans	3–4	1–6	1–4		8	23	0	4th

Division 3	Away team				Goals			
	R	A	C	S	F	A	Pts	Posn
Rovers		0–6	0–6	1–4	2	35	0	4th
Academicals	8–0		3–1	3–4	28	8	9	2nd
Casuals	4–1	2–2		1–6	17	16	5	3rd
Strollers	7–0	1–6	4–3		26	14	10	1st

With the scoring plan specified, this meant that the overall order of directors was: S (36 points); C and A (30 points); R (24 points).

97   The following example game shows five players using different tactics. Scrooge never sends to anyone, and just hopes that people will send enough to him. Wenceslas sends to everyone on the first go, and thereafter sends a card back to everyone from whom he received one last year, and sends with a 20% probability to those from whom he didn't receive a card. Caspar sends with a 50% probability to everyone in the first year, and after that replies to anyone from whom he has received a card in either of the last two years, but doesn't send any cards in the final year. Melchior sends with a 60% probability in the first year, and in subsequent years sends to each person with a probability equal to the proportion of years in which he has received cards from that person. Balthazar adopts a similar tactic but with a 70% probability in the first year, and doesn't send at all in the final two years.

The tables below show what happened over the ten years allotted, with cards being undelivered with a 10% probability. The row indicates who sent the card, and the column indicates whom it was sent to; an x means the card was received, while an o means that it was lost in the post.

	S	W	C	M	B
S	.	.	.	.	.
W	x	.	x	x	x
C	.	o	.	.	x
M	x	.	.	.	x
B	.	.	.	x	.

	S	W	C	M	B
S	.	.	.	.	.
W	.	.	x	.	.
C	.	x	.	.	.
M	.	x	.	.	x
B	.	x	x	.	.

	S	W	C	M	B
S	.	.	.	.	.
W	x	.	x	x	x
C	.	x	.	.	x
M	.	x	.	.	.
B	.	x	.	x	.

	S	W	C	M	B
S	.	.	.	.	.
W	.	.	x	x	x
C	.	x	.	.	o
M	.	x	.	.	x
B	.	x	x	x	.

	S	W	C	M	B
S	.	.	.	.	.
W	.	.	x	x	x
C	.	x	.	.	x
M	.	x	.	.	x
B	.	.	.	x	.

	S	W	C	M	B
S	.	.	.	.	.
W	.	.	o	x	.
C	.	x	.	.	x
M	.	x	.	.	x
B	.	x	.	x	.

	S	W	C	M	B
S	.	.	.	.	.
W	.	.	x	x	x
C	.	o	.	.	.
M	.	.	.	.	x
B	.	x	x	x	.

	S	W	C	M	B
S	.	.	.	.	.
W	.	.	.	.	x
C	.	x	.	.	x
M	.	x	.	.	.
B	.	x	x	x	.

	S	W	C	M	B
S	.	.	.	.	.
W	.	.	o	o	x
C	.	x	.	.	x
M	.	x	.	.	x
B	.	.	.	.	.

	S	W	C	M	B
S	.	.	.	.	.
W	x	.	o	x	.
C	.	.	.	.	.
M	.	x	.	.	x
B	.	.	.	.	.

Total	Sent	Recd	Points
Scrooge	0	4	12
Wenceslas	27	21	36
Caspar	16	10	14
Melchior	17	14	25
Balthazar	17	21	46

98 Here is an example game. The labelling of the rows and columns is given in the diagram, which also shows the position reached at the end of the example. Ordinary moves are shown in an obvious way; capture moves are indicated by '×' and are followed by 'sliding' moves shown in brackets and indicated by '\'.

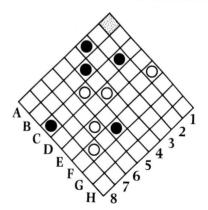

H4–F5	F8–E6
H6–G4	D8–C6
H2–F3	B8–A6
G4–E3	A6–B4
H3–F4	E8–C7
F4–E2	C7–B5
H5–F4	E6–C5
E2–D4	B5–A3
F3–E1	C6×D4
(D4\D7)	
F5×D4	(D4\G4)
(F4\F7)	G4×E3
(E3\E6)	
D7×C5	(C5\F5)
	E3–C2

(see diagram)

Black wins; he is threatening to win immediately, and can only be delayed by captures on C2, to which he can respond by recapturing immediately.

99   Here is an example game, with five counties playing each other twice each. The strategy of Ayshire is always to play safe. Beesex when batting first play safe for the first 50 balls, then take risks; when batting second they take risks if they have more than five wickets left or need fewer than 80 runs, but play safe otherwise. Ceeland when batting first take risks only when there are fewer than 100 balls left and they have scored fewer than 100 runs and they have more than five wickets left; when batting second they take risks only when they need more than 0.4 runs per ball. Deeset take risks for only the last 25 balls of the innings, whether batting first or second. Eefolk always play riskily.

Each entry in the table shows runs–wickets\balls. The row denotes the side batting first, and the column the side batting second. 'ao' denotes 'all out'.

	A	B	C	D	E
A		71–5\200 72–5\80	80–3\200 81–2\184	85–6\200 86–3\192	70–9\200 71–9\90
B	126ao\171 76–0\200		94ao\133 94–6\200	73ao\118 74–2\181	94ao\143 83ao\105
C	84–9\200 73–3\200	92–5\200 77ao\89		86–7\200 87–2\192	82–8\200 59ao\73
D	91–2\200 87–5\200	74–7\200 57ao\73	92–5\200 93–8\197		90–8\200 89ao\112
E	68ao\90 69–2\151	78ao\92 62ao\78	40ao\52 41–3\96	116ao\136 80–6\200	

With four points for a victory, Ceeland won with 26 points, then Deeset with 24, Beesex with 14, Eefolk with 12, and last was Ayshire with 4.

100   Here is an example game, in which the second player wins. White moves one of her pieces off at the first opportunity. Black then selects a sideways move which forces white into two sideways moves, enough to allow black to get both his pieces off first.

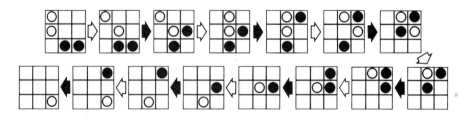

7 Solutions

STARTERS

1 If you spell out each digit, you will find that the last letter of each word is the first letter of the next. Therefore the only solution for the missing digit is 8.

2 One of the minimum-length solutions is BLACK, BLANK, BLINK, CLINK, CHINK, CHINE, WHINE, WHITE. There are others.

3 Take the nth number, add 1, and multiply by n, to get the next number each time. The answer is therefore 64.

4 The coding is A = 1, B = 3, C = 5, . . ., M = 25, N = 2, O = 4, . . ., Z = 26. The quotation is from Krishnamurti: 'If we can really understand the problem, the answer will come out of it, because the answer is not separate from the question.'

5 The series is the first letters of the planets, in order of increasing average distance from the Sun. The hint may have drawn your attention to the letters S, U, N, which of course throws light on the series. The answer is E for Earth.

6 One solution is HEAD, HELD, HELL, TELL, TALL, TAIL. Solutions with four intermediate steps, all of which are everyday words, use as steps HELD or HEAL, HELL or TEAL, HALL or TELL, and HAIL or TALL; these combine in a total of seven ways. If you found the obscure word indicated in the hints, you will have been able to find a shorter solution of HEAD, HEAL, TEAL, TAAL, TAIL.

7 There are twelve numbers in the series, as many as there are months in the year. If you write down each month, replace each letter with the number representing its position in the alphabet (so A = 1, B = 2, etc.), and add up the numbers for each month, you will get the numbers shown, with 103 as the missing number.

8 A score of 300 is good; 400 is very good; 500 is excellent. Possible long words are: eight letters – allspice, chenille, clannish, clanship, eggshell, especial, languish, lapillus, legalise, legalize, nuisance, penalise, penalize, pinnacle, pungence, salience, sapience, spillage; nine letters – challenge, peninsula; ten letters – changeling.

9   These are the numbers 0, 1, 2, ... typed on a calculator and turned upside-down. The next letter is therefore L.

10   Take each number, subtract the first digit, and add the second digit, to get the next number. This makes the solution 63. There is more about this in the next chapter.

11   The key word is ORTS. One solution is MARS, OARS, OATS, ORTS, ORES, ARES. There are three other solutions, involving MATS as the second word and/or ARTS as the fifth.

12   The sequence gives the second letters of the months of the year. The missing letters are thus P and C.

13   Both sums are $90 + 19 = 109$.

14   The letters are those which are normally written with three straight lines. The missing letter is therefore N.

15   BRICK, TRICK, THICK, THINK, THINE, SHINE, SHONE, STONE is one solution.

16   361, 529, 784 (the squares of 19, 23 and 28).

17   Each of the numbers is the smallest positive whole number for which the name uses a certain number of letters. The next two numbers are 73 and 3000, because SEVENTY-THREE and THREE THOUSAND are the smallest numbers needing twelve and thirteen letters respectively. There is more on this topic in the next chapter.

18   HERA, HERD, HARD, HARK, HANK, HUNK, JUNK, JUNO. You could also have the pair HERE and HARE instead of the pair HERD and HARD.

THE ADVENTURES OF THE SEVEN DWARFS

19   Add two consecutive numbers and subtract 1 to get the next number (the sequence is therefore one more than the Fibonacci sequence). The next number is thus 9, and the letter nine places before E in the alphabet is V.

20   The birds, with some surrounding text, are: deeD OVEr with; rEGRETted; awFUL MARriage; deeP LOVE Remained; comPEL, I CANnot; whether I DO? DOubtless; seCOND OR two; the truTH, RUSHed away; left HER ON her own; loST IN The woods; bRAVE, Not knowing; hER NExt move; a BITTER Night; the rain beGAN. NETtles abounded; forMER LINen sheets; a disMAL LARDer; a tREE VEry good; falling fasTER Now; faster nOW, Leaving; was GOD WITh her? (tHEN is not strictly a type of bird, just the female sex of fowl in general.)

21   The number of feet is the number of vowels in their names (Y doesn't strictly count as a vowel); the number of inches is the position of their initial in the

alphabet. 'Nominal' in the hint means 'relating to name'. So Dozey is 2 feet 4 inches, Grumpy is 1 foot 7 inches and Doc is 1 foot 4 inches tall.

22   Snow White. Dopey, Hairy and Doc hold four, four and three diamonds in some order; Dozey and Jock have two and three spades, respectively, but they can't hold the ace, king or queen because their spades are the same as their clubs, and Grumpy has these cards in clubs. Since only four people have spades, the two apart from Dozey and Jock must have four each, and so can only be Bossy and Snow White. So the ace, king and queen of spades are held by Bossy and Snow White; but supposing Bossy held the queen, he would also have to have the ace and king, because otherwise Snow White would hold a higher court card. Then Bossy holds three court cards and Snow White cannot exceed this (the most she could have would be the jack of spades and two courts in either hearts or spades). Therefore, this contradicts the conditions and our supposition was wrong, which means Snow White must hold the queen of spades.

23   Each dwarf looked at the lengths of the names of the two dwarfs opposite him, and formed the number from the two lengths. So Jock saw Dopey and Dozey, each with five letters in his name, and formed the number 55.

24   Jock was in Grumpy's room. The rest of the sorry situation was that Grumpy was in Bossy's, Bossy was in Dozey's, Dozey was in Doc's, Doc was in Hairy's, Hairy was in Dopey's, and Dopey was in Jock's.

25   Jock led it, and in fact Jock was also the only one who told the truth.

26   Dopey started his leave on the second Wednesday. The arrangement had to be that Hairy and Grumpy had one and four days off (although you can't tell which of the two had which), Doc had six, Jock had two, Bossy had three, Dozey had seven and Dopey had five.

27   There were 32 chunks, and the slab had been in the cupboard for 3 days 18 hours.

28   The picture shows the basket as Snow White saw it at the end, and Hairy chose the eight shaded apples. These are the only eight unpoisoned apples. The one which Snow White had chosen at the beginning of the first 'episode' was the leftmost of the middle row; the one she had chosen at the beginning of the second 'episode' was the middle of the row now nearest her.

Snow White

29

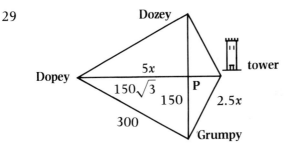

The diagram shows the distances in feet, where x is the height of the tower. Conditions are identical for Dozey and Grumpy, so the line from Dopey to the tower is the perpendicular bisector of the line between Dozey and Grumpy, meeting it at a point labelled P in the diagram. The distances from P to Grumpy and from P to Dopey are therefore as shown in the diagram, because they are parts of a 30°–60°–90° triangle. Then, using Pythagoras on the triangle formed by P, Grumpy and the tower, the equation $x^2 - 80\sqrt{3}x + 4800 = 0$ is obtained. This has a repeated root of $x = 40\sqrt{3}$, so to the nearest foot the height of the tower is 69 feet.

30 At 6:08 Grumpy found the noose, which had been placed on Thursday.
At 6:10 Bossy found the weight, which had been place on Tuesday.
At 6:12 Jock found the spikes, which had been placed on Friday.
At 6:17 Doc found the magnifying glass, which had been placed on Saturday.
At 6:21 Hairy found the explosives, which had been placed on Wednesday.
At 6:26 Dozey found the scorpion, which had been placed on Monday.
At 6:28 Dopey noticed the saw-cuts, which had been made on Sunday.

31 The large square had 127 people on each side; the small squares had 48 on each side. $127^2 = 7 \times 48^2 + 1$ is the total size of the army; that is, 16 129.

32 Suitable formulae that give the required number, 48, are (in the order stated):

$D + P + Y + O/E$ $[Z \times (Y - O)/E] - D$
$P \times (Y - M)/(G + R - U)$ $C \times (K + O - J)$
$(Y - S) \times (S - O) \times B$ $[H \times (Y - R)] - I + A$
$D \times (O - C)$

Other solutions are possible.

33 One of the possible solutions is shown below.

   B D F   G D A   G F C
  A C E G   B F C E   D A E B

   F A D   B C A   C D E   D A E
  C B E G   E G F D   A G B F   F B G C

34 The road is 3.5 miles long, and the dwarfs travel on it at one-fifth of 50, i.e. at ten miles an hour. The diagonal route is 2.5 miles, and they move on that at one-half of fifteen, i.e. at seven and a half miles an hour. Therefore the road takes 21 minutes, but they chose the quicker way across the fields, taking 20 minutes.

35 GEBCFAD

36 The quickest route for the prince would have been first left, second left, second left. The map of the relevant region of the woods is shown in the diagram.

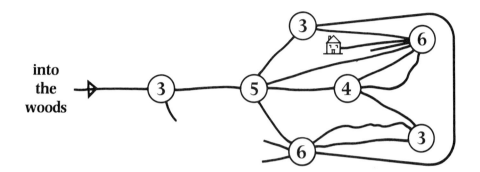

37 Dopey, Doc and Jock, respectively. The full situation was: Grumpy bought the chocolates and wanted to hold hands; Dopey bought the tulips and wanted to look from a distance; Hairy bought the crocuses and wanted to walk with her; Dozey bought the daisies and wanted to stroke her hair; Bossy bought the daffodils and wanted to gaze into her eyes; Jock bought the freesias and wanted to kiss her; Doc bought the violets and wanted to sit with her.

38 The full situation was as follows: Hairy is Colin, and he had no tea and was lying; Jock is Martin, and he had tea and told the truth; Grumpy is Ian, and he had no tea and was lying; Doc is Keith, and he had no tea and told the truth; Bossy is Gordon, and he had tea and told the truth; Dopey is Neil, and he had tea and was lying; Dozey is Barry, and he had no tea and told the truth.

THE ISLE OF MARANGA

39 The cycles of temperature, wind and precipitation as listed start in July, March and November, respectively. That fits the conditions given, and makes my favourite month June.

40 The population in 1902 was 50 000, with 40% men, 25% women, 20% boys and 15% girls. In 1952 the population of 80 000 comprised 30% men, 45% women, 15% boys and 10% girls. The numbers of women were 12 500 in 1902 and 36 000 in 1952.

41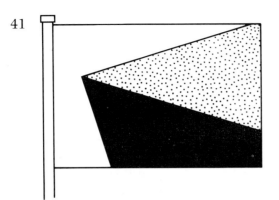

The three points are 34 chisen along the top edge from the hoist; 18 chisen down the fly from the top; 10 chisen along the bottom edge from the hoist. The flag therefore appears as illustrated.

42   The longest interval is 1064 days, and that last occurred between 2 February 1966 and 1 January 1969. The shortest interval is incidentally 175 days, and that last occurred between 9 September 1981 and 3 March 1982. Before that, the shortest interval was between those dates in 1970 and 1971. These three interval extremes, one long and two short, repeat every 28 years as stated in the hint.

43   Orange means that you may proceed in any direction. Violet means that you may go left or straight, or if nothing is coming then to the right also. Turquoise means that left only is allowed, and puce means stop. Therefore in the diagrams in the puzzle, only cars numbered 1, 4 and 7 may proceed.

44   Signpost 1 belongs in Cellawa, and Wertso is the missing name. No. 2 belongs in Gyra, with Cellawa missing. No. 3 is for Tuvo, with Spranso missing. No. 4 is for Spranso, with Cellawa missing. No. 5 belongs in Blimpscoe, with Rackle missing. No. 6 is for Wertso, with Cellawa missing. No. 7 is for Rackle, with Aytow missing. No. 8 belongs to Aytow, with Spranso the missing name. A map of the signposted region is shown in the diagram (you may have drawn it with any of the 'faces' of the map as the exterior one, but all such drawings give the same answer).

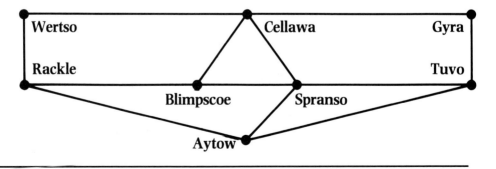

45 There are 144 rooms in all. The first 140 are different even if we ignore the type of glass, and then the pattern repeats. Rooms 1–4 have plain glass and rooms 141–144 frosted, but room 145 would have plain glass and so be exactly like room 5. Rooms 47 and 46 exchanged drapes, but 47 is not then quite like 102 because the glazing is different. The only pair that become identical are rooms 46 and 131.

46 The peal is: semibreve BD; minim C; quaver A; crotchet BC; dotted crotchet AD; quaver B; crotchet CD; dotted crotchet AB; minim D; semibreve AC.

47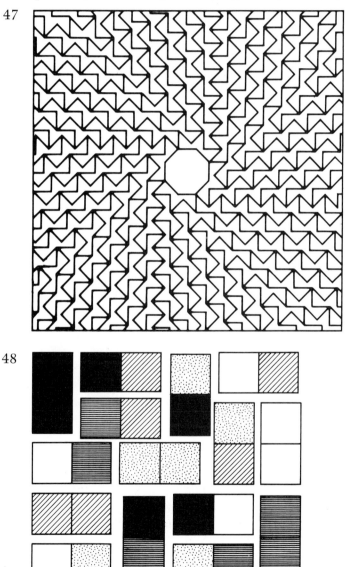

48

49

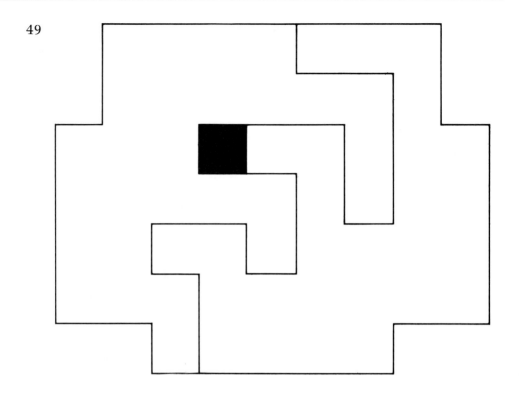

50

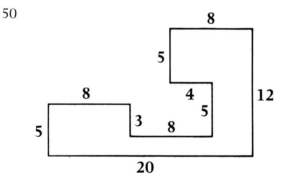

51 There are 62 precops in a versil, and 28 versils in an arpep. The change will thus be 1 arpep 3 versils 45 precops, and the item is worth £4.20.

52 The coins are worth 11, 4 and 2 precops. I received $11+11+4+2$ and $11+4+2+2+2$ on the two occasions.

53 There are 61 mathofs in a grunolf, and therefore 3721 square mathofs in a square grunolf. My acquaintance's estate is 15 grunolfs 60 mathofs on each side, having an area of 255 square grunolfs 1770 square mathofs.

54 Tarnop's birthplace and burial place are shown on the map, with all the irrelevant landmarks removed. The total distance travelled on his journeys is approximately 184 grunolfs.

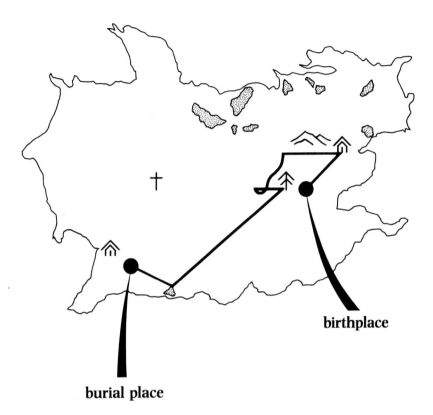

birthplace

burial place

55 The mystical sets are:
        amulet, bangle, chalice
        amulet, bangle, drakestone;
        amulet, chalice, drakestone;
        amulet, drakestone, flagon;
        amulet, emblem, flagon;
        bangle, chalice, drakestone, flagon;
        bangle, drakestone, emblem;
        bangle, emblem, flagon;
        chalice, emblem, flagon;
        drakestone, emblem, flagon.

56   St Tarnop chose the drakestone.

Then if Hastaman had chosen the amulet, he would have taken the emblem, and on his last turn either the bangle or the flagon.

Or if Hastaman had taken the bangle, he would have taken the flagon, and then the amulet or the emblem.

If Hastaman had taken the chalice, he could have taken the amulet, and then any remaining item.

If Hastaman had taken the emblem, he would have taken the amulet, and then any remaining item.

If Hastaman had taken the flagon, he could have taken the amulet, and then either the bangle or the chalice.

Any starting choice other than the drakestone would have lost.

If Tarnop had chosen the amulet, Hastaman could have taken the drakestone, and then countered the bangle with the chalice and vice versa, and the emblem with the flagon and vice versa.

If he had taken the bangle, Hastaman could have taken the drakestone, and then countered the amulet with the chalice and vice versa, and the emblem with the flagon and vice versa.

If he had taken the chalice, Hastaman could have taken the amulet, and then either the emblem or the flagon.

If Tarnop had started with the emblem, Hastaman could have taken the flagon, and then either the bangle or the drakestone.

If Tarnop had taken the flagon, Hastaman could have taken the emblem, and then either the amulet or the drakestone.

57   The area of the shield was 32 times the area of the last piece. The only run of consecutive primes which sums to a multiple of 32 that is less than 1000 is $2+3+5+7+11+13+17+19+23+29+31=160$. Since $5=160/32$, 5 is the last piece, and on the fourth stroke 2 and 13 must have fallen. On the third stroke 3 and 17 must have fallen, and on the second 11 and 29 must have fallen.

58   The only possibility is that the total number of jewels is 684, Nogdor came to the throne when he was 27, and celebrated his last anniversary when he was 45. Since he died just before his next anniversary, he had reigned for nearly 18 years.

59   The Archdukes', Barons' and Commoners' courts met at intervals of five, three and eight years respectively. The relevant meetings must have been when Olnic had reigned for 55, 57, 64, 66 and 70 years, i.e. his reign overall lasted 70 years.

60   Hetik ruled for 14 years and 72 days. $72^2=14\times365+74$, so if there are exactly two 29 February days during his reign, this sum works correctly. Since he must have gained the throne on 20 October 1688, these would have been in 1692 and 1696 only, so the solution is correct.

61   There are eight combinations of arrangements of the houses in our and their dating systems. Each of these imposes conditions on the amounts of the shifts of dates. The given shifts only satisfy the conditions for one of these combinations: the one where the order of the houses is Switheroe 1763–94 (1703–34), Beresoul 1744–62 (1735–53), Switheroe 1814–45 (1754–85), Beresoul 1795–1813 (1786–1804), Eresord 1703–43 (1805–45). There is more on this problem in the next chapter.

62   The reigns are: Tramin I 1846–79, his son Rybar 1879–93, his son Ani I 1893–96, his brother Elni I 1896–1907, his uncle Elni II 1907–30, his brother Ani II 1930–38, his brother Tramin II 1938–61, his son Elni III 1961–78, and his son Elni IV 1978–date.

63   The notes of the first, second, third and fourth strings open must be D, A, F, C♯, so that the first fingering gives the notes in the order A, D, C, F♯ and the second fingering gives D, B, G, E if the second string is stopped at the second fret.

64   The three valves increase the pitch by 2, 3 and 7 semitones. The eight possible fingerings then raise the basic pitch by 0, 2, 3, 5, 7, 9, 10 or 12 semitones, which gives eight consecutive notes in the scale of C major as long as the lowest note is D.

65   Damper 1 cuts out C♯, D, D♯, F, F♯, A, A♯; damper 2 cuts out D, F, G♯, B; damper 3 cuts out C, D♯, F♯, G, A♯; damper 4 cuts out C♯, E, G, A. The major chord that dampers 1 and 3 together produce is E major (E, G♯, B); dampers 3 and 4 together produce D diminished (D, F, G♯, B); dampers 2 and 4 together produce D♯ minor sixth (D♯, F♯, A♯, C). Dampers 1 and 4 together allow C, G♯ and B to sound.

66   The arrangement of notes in the basic pattern is as shown in the diagram. (Of course, the F♯ in the third row is in the octave below the F further along the third row.)

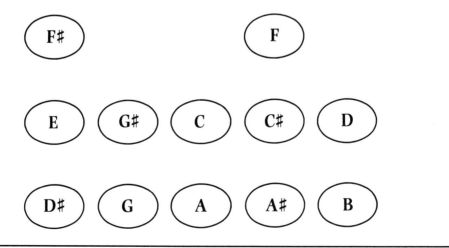

THE MARTIAN DATING AGENCY AND OTHER PROBLEMS

67   The triples are: Ag,Nop,Sed; Bik, Ob,Vod; Cag,Pib,Wot; Deg,Lep,Tid; Eck,Mib,Ut.

68   The other two parents are shown in the diagram. The mother, Bep, has green peepers, a flat hooter, violet fur and short antennae; the nuther, Ced, has red peepers, a flared hooter, pink fur and long antennae. Dor is male and El is female.

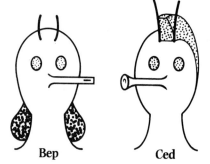

Bep   Ced

69   Forward is achieved by a three of MLR or MRL followed or preceded by a five of MLODA or MRAGO, which gives eight combinations. Left is achieved by MRDA or MRAR. Right is achieved by MLGO or MLOL. The six basic positions, and the steps which lead from one to another, are shown in the diagram. The numale's feet positions are indicated by x and the female's by o; a little rotation is sometimes needed to see how one leads to another.

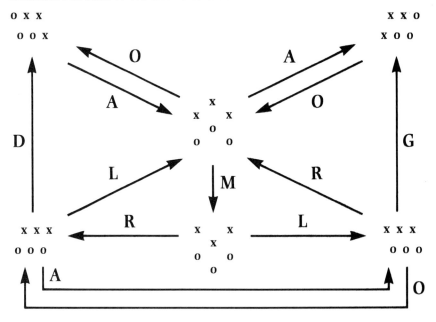

70   The only possible teams are:

The Droopy Antennae   Aik, Cug, Hig and Lek;
The Flat Hooters   Bak, Eeg, Gok and Ick;
The Violet Furs   Dak, Feg, Jeg and Kig.

71   Ellen Nicholas, Colette O'Neill, Joanna Phillips, Geraldine Qureshi, Bronwen Raje, Isabel Sewell, Alison Tan, Hazel Uddin, Florence Victor, Doris Williams.

72   Gary. The full count was: Alice 4, Bill 7, Catherine 2, Dave 10, Edward 5, Frances 11, Gary 6, Henry 3, Irene 8, Kevin 9, Lucy 1.

73   The order of the charts was WUYTVZX. The two 'irregular' records were 'Even when you try' and 'Nobody else'.

74   The gateau was 6 cm wide, 12 cm high and 20 cm long.

75   Using the algebra suggested in the hint, you need to solve $(x-d)(y-d)=d(2d-1)$. Each bracket could still have a number of factorizations, but if you try $x-d=d$ and $y-d=2d-1$ for various values of d you will find the only possible solution in the last hundred or so years. Since $1976 = 2 \times 26 \times 38$, and $1989 = 39 \times 51$, I must have met her in 1989 when she was 13.

76   Adding $a+b/c$ and $b+a/c$ and subtracting $(a+b)/c$ gives you $a+b$; so $a+b=20$. It is then straightforward to find b, and then a and c. The answer is that $a=8$, $b=12$, $c=4$, and he should have typed $8+12=/4=$.

77   The coding is:

A   B   C   D   E   F   G   H   I   J   K   L   M
3   +   4   5   −   7   8   /   2   ×   1   9   6

The answer to the ultimate expression is then $46-4$, so equals 42, or CI.

78   (a) $9902 = 2 \times 4951$, which gives 4773;
(b) $1909 = 23 \times 83$, which gives 86.

79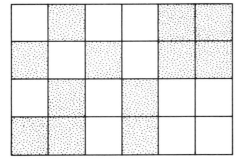

80   The longest ride found is of length 46, as shown.

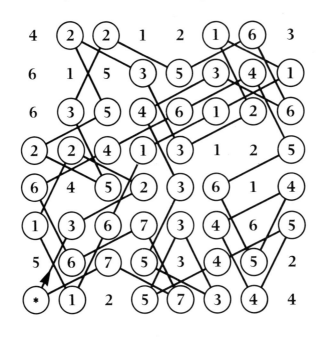

81

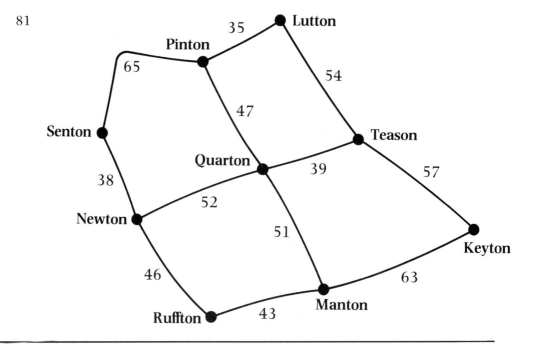

82   The best known solution is shown, with a shortest crack of length 31. There is more on this problem in the next chapter.

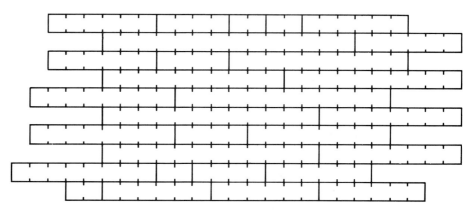

83   Along the route you should have gathered the numbers 11, 29, 30, 33, 83, which multiply together to give 26 212 230. If you guess that the signs at the entrance and exit spell IN and OUT respectively, you can deduce that the numbers should be taken two digits at a time and decoded by $8 = A$, $9 = B$, $10 = C, \ldots, 33 = Z$. This gives the password as SNOW.

84   Five horses are needed, and this minimum number gets you round in the smallest number of moves. Each horse can only ever reach one-fifth of the squares. In a similar way that in chess each bishop can only get to squares of one of the two colours, you could colour the squares of the course with five colours so that each horse can only land on one colour. Taking any one particular horse, it needs an adjacent horse of each of the other four colours in order to move in each of the four possible directions, so certainly at least five horses are necessary. When you consider the minimum number of moves each horse could conceivably take to get round, you will see that the total below cannot be bettered with more than five horses.

       The solution below is the shortest that has been found. The starting positions are B12, C12, B11, C11, D11. The square a horse leaves from on any move need not be given, because each time there is only one horse that could move there. The destinations of successive moves are: D10, C10, B10, D9, C9, B9, D8, C8, B8, D7, C7, D9, E7, E6, D6, C6, E5, D5, E7, F5, F4, E4, F6, G4, G3, F3, G5, H5, H4, H3, I5, I4, I3, J5, J4, J3, K5, K4, K3, L5, L4, L3, M5, M4, M3, N5, N4, L5, N6, O6, O5, M6, O7, P7, P6, N7, P8, Q8, Q7, Q6, R7, R8, P8, R9, Q9, P9, Q10, P10, P8, O10, O11, P11, Q11, P12, O12, O10, N12, N11, N10, M11, M10, O10, M9, L9, L10, L11, K10, K9, M9, M8, L8, K8, L7, M7, M9, N7, N6, M6, L6, N5, M5, L5, M4, N4, N6, O4, O3, N3, M3, O2, N2. That's a total of 111 moves.

SPORTS AND GAMES

85   The Overnet line-up was: goalkeeper – 3; defenders – 10, 11; midfield – 6, 7, 8; forwards – 1, 2, 4, 5, 9. The Veropolli line-up was: goalkeeper – 6; defenders – 1, 2, 4, 5; midfield – 7, 8, 9; forwards – 3, 10, 11.

86   The best possible score is 27 strokes, or nine under par. Suitable plays are given below, although there are alternatives of equal lengths in some cases.

   Hole 1:   3 strokes – start from the east square on the tee, then go 7 east, 5 east, 2 east.
   Hole 2:   2 strokes – from west square, 6 north-east, 3 south-east.
   Hole 3:   4 strokes — from north-west square, 9 north-west, 6 west, 3 west, 1 south-east.
   Hole 4:   4 strokes – from centre square, 8 north-east, 7 east, 3 north-east, 1 south-west.
   Hole 5:   3 strokes — from north-west square, 9 south-east, 5 north-east, 6 south-east.
   Hole 6:   2 strokes – from west square, 6 east, 5 north-east.
   Hole 7:   3 strokes – from centre square, 7 south-east, 6 north-east, 5 south-east.
   Hole 8:   3 strokes – from south-west square, 9 west, 5 north-east, 7 north-west.
   Hole 9:   3 strokes – from north-east square, 9 east, 6 north-east, 4 south-east.

87   The points achieved by the teams each season were:

Season	1	2	3	4	5	6	7	8	9	10	11	12
Grange United	4	4	2	2	3	3	1	1	4	4	2	2
Cartmel Wanderers	1	2	4	3	2	4	3	4	1	2	1	4
Alithwaite Academicals	2	1	1	4	4	2	4	3	3	1	4	1
Lindale Town	3	3	3	1	1	1	2	2	2	3	3	3

   The positions at the end of the ninth season were therefore Grange United, then Alithwaite Academicals, then Lindale Town, then Cartmel Wanderers.

88   (a) 143 (45 + 48 + 50); (b) 151 (e.g. 57 + 54 + 40); (c) there is none.

89   Jones won by 0–6, 7–5, 6–3, 6–7, 14–12.

90   One possibility is ABD, CEF, ABC, ACE for the venues. If A, B, C and E qualify then they could go to the venues in five orders: ACBE, AEBC, BCAE, BEAC, BECA. There is a little more on this question in the next chapter.

91   Olive backed   no. 4,   Desert Rose,   which finished 1st.
Ian backed   no. 3,   Escarmouche, which finished 2nd.
Nigel backed   no. 6,   Burnt Oak   which finished 3rd.
John backed   no. 1,   Aldini,   which finished 4th.
Leslie backed   no. 2,   Fountain,   which finished 5th.
Mandy backed   no. 7,   Gregale,   which finished 6th.
Ken backed   no. 5,   Curl,   which finished 7th.

92   No, Plant did not win 76–71. If that's what you've got, then you've made several correct deductions, but there's a slight catch to this question. If you've come here straight from the question, then try again. Stop reading this and rethink, or have a look at the hint.

     The point is that the highest joint total without penalties is not 147. A situation can come about when the game finishes as a draw, and the black has to be respotted. This needs an even total when all the usual balls have been potted, and the highest for that is 146, with one of the reds being followed by pink as the bonus ball, and the rest with black. The overall total will then be 153. The only such way which satisfies the conditions stated is for Potter to win 80–73, by potting seven reds with blacks, plus brown, pink, black and the respotted black; Plant pocketed seven reds with blacks, one red with a pink, plus yellow, green and blue. (If you had wrongly taken 147 as the highest possible joint total, the conditions would have suggested that Plant won by 76–71.)

93   It is extremely complicated to make a full analysis of the game as it was stated. An analysis can, though, be done for small versions of the game.

     If we have only three numbers (instead of eleven) totalling 5 (instead of 100), with the numbers having to differ by more than 1 (instead of more than 2), then there are two basic strategies: play the 4,1,0 and 3,2,0 and 2,2,1 formations with equal frequencies; or play the 3,2,0 and 3,1,1 and 2,2,1 formations in the ratio 2 : 1 : 2. In both cases the particular formation should be chosen at random each time, and then the actual order of the formation (e.g. 2,2,1 or 2,1,2 or 1,2,2) should be randomized. As an added refinement, the two basic strategies can be mixed in any ratio.

     With three numbers totalling 6, the numbers having to differ by more than 1, there are again two basic strategies: one is to play the 4,2,0 formation; the other is to play the 4,1,1 and 3,3,0 and 2,2,2 formations with equal frequency. Again, the actual order should be randomized, and the two strategies can be mixed in any ratio.

     With three numbers totalling 7, numbers having to differ by more than 1 to score, yet again there are two basic strategies that can be mixed: play the 4,3,0 and 4,2,1 and 3,2,2 formations with equal frequency; or play the 3,3,1 and 4,2,1 and 3,2,2 formations with equal frequency.

94   Without making a complete analysis of this, it is still possible to present a few observations. As X, say, you must not let your opponent fill a column with Os, or he or she will choose that column in the last phase and win. Also, you can often look ahead to the final grid arrangement and see that you can rule out one of your rows, while your opponent rules out one of his or her columns. If you can't then rule out another row or column, a rule of thumb is that the grid favours the players in proportion to the number of symbols they have in that 2×2 sub-grid (i.e. they will be equal, or one side will have a $2:1$ advantage).

95   The moral of this game is that you shouldn't raise the prize unless you're very likely to win – only bet on (near) certainties! An analysis of your expected winning amount shows that you should never raise unless you are within one throw of winning, and unless your opponent is not. The table below indicates when you should raise in terms of your score, your opponent's score, and the current prize.

		Opponent's score							
		0	1	2	3	4	5	6	7
	9	A	A	A	A	A	8	4	X
Your score	8	A	A	A	A	5	2	1	X
	7	A	A	6	3	1	X	X	X
	6	X	X	X	X	X	X	X	X

A = always raise.   X = never raise.
Number = raise if the stake is less than or equal to that number.

The game can be adapted by choosing other totals, or allowing unlimited raising of stakes, or using other methods of scoring. For instance, you could use just one coin and score 0 or 1 with equal chances each time; or use a die and score from 1 to 6.

96   There are three elements to this game: allocating the strengths to the three divisions; dividing up each team's strength into attack, midfield and defence; and luck! The first of these is not straightforward to analyse in a multi-player game, so it is left for you to experiment; the second does have a definite best method; for the third, you have to hope.

The essential aspect of an individual game comes down to two probabilities: the chances of one team scoring two goes after the ball is in midfield, and the chance of the other team doing so. If either team scores in these two moves, the ball returns to midfield for the kick-off; and if neither does, then the ball must have gone one way, then the other, and ended up in midfield anyway. So the ball is in the same position every two moves whatever happens, and the game reduces to ten iterations of: does the first team score?; does the second team score?; does neither team score?

If attack/midfield/defence are $a/b/c$ and $d/e/f$ for the two teams, then on any one occasion the chance of the first team scoring is $[a/(a+f)] \times [b/(b+e)]$, and the chance of the second team scoring is $[d/(c+d)] \times [e/(b+e)]$. It is not hard to prove that the best allocation of strengths is to have equal values for attack and defence, with midfield being twice that value (limited by the maximum allowed, if that is applicable). The restriction of having to use whole numbers will stop this being achievable always, but this is the theoretical best.

97 The basis of this game involves two mathematical paradoxes: the 'prisoner's dilemma' and the 'unexpected hanging'. These have been discussed in books on recreational mathematics (chapter 29 of Douglas Hofstadter's *Metamagical Themas*, and chapter 1 of Martin Gardner's *Further Mathematical Diversions*, both of which are compilations of *Scientific American* columns). The lesson of the former is that you should start off sending cards to everyone, and in subsequent years you should send cards to those who sent to you in the previous year. However, the game as stated, with cards randomly going astray, complicates this; you could take the view that you should be slightly forgiving, in case a card to you was sent but not received; alternatively, you could assume that you can get away with not sending a card to someone occasionally, expecting him or her to believe that your card has got lost in the post.

The 'unexpected hanging' part of the game occurs because all the players know when the game will end. Everyone will surely assume that they shouldn't send a card in the final year, because there's no time afterwards for anyone to default in retaliation. Then, knowing that no-one will send you a card in the final year, what's the point in your sending any in the penultimate year? Therefore no-one will send any that year either, and so on inductively backwards, so that no-one ever sends any. And yet if I send you a card in the first year and you also send me one, we'll score more highly than those Scrooges who followed the argument and never sent any. So where's the flaw in the argument?

The game, probably more than any of the others in this book, requires practical experiment. So try it, and see what successful tactics people come up with!

98 It is left to the reader to investigate the standard game, and find out which player has the win. In the one-piece-per-side game, though, where the starting position

is symmetrical, the diagram shows which player should win. If the players start symmetrically on dark squares, the first player has the win; if they start symmetrically on white squares, the second player has the win. The shaded squares along the diagonal cannot be starting squares, because each one is symmetrical with itself.

99   It is interesting to use trial and error on this, especially with a computer, but tactics can be arrived at after some mathematical investigation. The following are put forward as simple but very effective tactics; if you can beat them consistently, well done!

(a)   If batting first, play safely if the number of balls left exceeds 20 times the number of wickets left; otherwise play riskily.

(b)   If batting second, play safely if the number of balls left exceeds 1.4 times the number of runs behind plus twice the number of wickets left; otherwise play riskily.

There is more on this game in the next chapter.

100   'Dodgem' has been mentioned in books on recreational mathematics. See chapter 12 of Martin Gardner's *Time Travel and Other Mathematical Bewilderments*, and chapter 22 (in volume 2) of Berlekamp, Conway and Guy's *Winning Ways*. The game on the 3×3 board is known to be a win for the first player, but the outcome on the 4×4 board has not been exhaustively analysed. *Winning Ways* has a table showing the outcome from any position on the 3×3 board, which implicitly indicates the best moves. It is entertaining to play against a partner to discover winning tactics for yourself. Although the idea of getting your corner piece to the main diagonal before your opponent does is a strong tactic, it is far from being the whole story, and there are several subtleties to negotiate before you can be sure of winning.

8 Coda

And suppose we solve all the problems it presents? What happens? We end up with more problems than we started with. Because that's the way problems propagate their species. A problem left to itself dries up or goes rotten. But fertilize a problem with a solution – you'll hatch out dozens.

N.F. Simpson, *A Resounding Tinkle*

This chapter doesn't contain any new problems, but it looks at extensions to a few from the previous chapters. Where there are still questions to be answered, they will generally be open-ended, and they are just presented as topics that might interest you, and they may be pursued as far or as little as you please.

10   For our next number

The solution to puzzle no. 10 was to take each number, subtract the first digit and add the second digit, to get the next number. This means that any number with the first and second digits equal will generate itself. Apart from these, though, every number generates a sequence that eventually leads to the loop 45, 46, 48, 52, 49, 54, 53, 51, 47, 50, 45, . . .

The problem can be generalized to two-digit numbers in any number base. The behaviour then varies, and not everything ends in the same non-trivial loop. For instance, in base 5, we obtain 01, 02, 04, 13, 20, 13, . . . and 23, 24, 31, 24, . . .

The pattern of behaviour in base n becomes apparent if each number is expressed in base $n+1$, curiously enough.

If $N = m(n+1) + r$ where $0 \leqslant r < n+1$, then the successor to N is $m'(n+1) + r'$, where $r' = 2r$ (modulo $n+1$), and

$$m' = m+1 \qquad \text{if } 2r > n \text{ and } m+r < n \tag{1}$$
$$m' = m-1 \qquad \text{if } 2r \leqslant n \text{ and } m+r \geqslant n \tag{2}$$
$$m' = m \qquad \text{otherwise} \tag{3}$$

This is fairly straightforward to prove. N as shown above can be rewritten as $mn + (m+r)$.

If $m+r<n$ then m and $m+r$ will be the two digits of the number, and so the successor is $mn+(m+r)-m+m+r=m(n+1)+2r$. If $2r<n+1$ then this fits the condition (3) above. If, on the other hand, $2r\geqslant n+1$ then the successor can be written as $(m+1)(n+1)+2r-(n+1)$, which fits condition (1).

If $m+r\geqslant n$ then $N=(m+1)n+(m+r-n)$ and the two digits are thus $m+1$ and $m+r-n$, so the successor is:

$$(m+1)n+(m+r-n)-(m+1)+(m+r-n)=m(n+1)+2r-(n+1)$$

If $2r\geqslant n+1$ this fits condition (3). If instead $2r<n+1$ then it can be written as $(m-1)(n+1)+2r$, which fits condition (2).

This theorem has the immediate consequence that when $m=(n-1)/2$ for n odd, or $m=(n-2)/2$ for n even, then $m'=m$ whatever the value of r. This happens because if $2r>n$ then $m+r\geqslant n$, and vice versa, so that condition (3) must always apply.

For certain numbers n the sequence behaves in a particularly interesting way. This happens when 2 is a primitive root of $n+1$. By this is meant that, if we start with 1 and keep doubling it, reducing modulo $n+1$ when appropriate, then we run through all the non-zero numbers up to n before returning to 1. In that case the numbers between $m+1$ and $m+n$, where $m=(n-1)/2$ or $(n-2)/2$ as appropriate, form a loop of length n. This is, in fact, the only non-trivial loop, and all sequences (other than the trivial ones starting at multiples of $n+1$) end up there.

To see this, consider what happens to a general $N=m(n+1)+r$. For any m other than the one which forms the loop, there is at least one r for which condition (1) holds if m is less than the 'special' value, and at least one r for which condition (2) holds if m is more than the special value. Also, (2) cannot hold if m is less than the value, and (1) cannot hold if m is more than the value.

Therefore, any sequence will stick with a particular value of m, with the r values cycling through the numbers from 1 to n (in some order) until an r is hit for which condition (3) does not hold, and then a new value of m will be taken which is nearer by 1 to the special value. Thus eventually the special value will be reached, and the sequence will be trapped in the loop.

It just happens that 10 is one of the values of n for which this behaviour occurs. The numbers less than 100 for which it occurs are 2, 4, 10, 12, 18, 28, 36, 52, 58, 60, 66, 82.

The problem can also be generalized to numbers with more than two digits. If we start with a number with d digits, subtract off the number formed by the first e digits, and add the number formed by the last e digits, we get another d-digit number and can repeat the process. The overall behaviour is more complicated, with the most interesting situation seeming to be when $e=d-1$.

For instance, with three-digit numbers, and subtracting and adding two-digit numbers (i.e. $d=3$, $e=2$), we can make the following list of number bases, non-trivial loop lengths, and typical loop elements:

base	2	one of length 4	010
base	3	one of length 8	110
base	4	one of length 4	201
base	5	two of length 2	132, 312
		one of length 8	210
base	6	one of length 2	310
		one of length 4	240
		one of length 6	232
base	7	two of length 2	251, 415
		two of length 7	253, 413
base	8	two of length 6	367, 410
base	9	two of length 2	367, 521
		two of length 5	328, 560
		two of length 8	427, 461
base	10	one of length 4	509
		one of length 6	528
		six of length 7	381, 618, 436, 563, 492, 507

As another investigation, you can work out for a particular case how two different numbers must be related if they have the same successor. This needs only a little bit of algebra. For instance, for $d=3$, $e=2$ as shown above, the numbers a, b, c and $a+p, b+q, c+r$ in base n will both have the same successor when $(n^2-n)p+(2n-1)q+2r=0$. This can be solved (with p, q and r being anything between $1-n$ and $n-1$) to tell you the possible differences between digits.

17   The table of Babel

Puzzle no. 17 turned out to be about the smallest numbers in English which require a certain number of letters in their expressions. There are no numbers with one or two letters in their expressions, so the series starts one, four, three, eleven, fifteen, thirteen, seventeen, twenty-four.

Different languages show different characteristics in relation to this question. Most languages progress reasonably smoothly. The English jump from 73 to 3000 is one of the most startling, but, as you will see below, there is a language with a bigger jump, and also languages that start and then have gaps of a few places for which there are no corresponding numbers.

In the event of this book doing so well that it has to be translated into foreign languages, the sequences in most European languages are shown in the table below. Accents and diacritic marks have been omitted, and note that in transliterating from Russian the word length changes.

Smallest number containing number of letters

Language	Two	Three	Four	Five	Six	Seven	Eight	Nine	Ten
English	—	1 one	4 four	3 three	11 eleven	15 fifteen	13 thirteen	17 seventeen	24 twenty-four
Cornish	—	2 deu	1 onen	6 whegh	4 peswar	12 deudhek	60 tryugans	14 peswardek	50 hanter cans
Czech	—	2 dva	6 sest	1 jeden	20 dvacet	12 dvanact	11 jedenact	22 dvacet dve	19 devatenact
Danish	1 en	3 tre	4 fire	18 atten	11 elleve	13 tretten	21 enogtyve	23 treogtyve	24 fireogtyve
Dutch	—	1 een	2 twee	7 zeven	12 twaalf	13 dertien	14 veertien	17 zeventien	101 honderd een
Esperanto	2 du	1 unu	4 kvar	12 dek du	11 dek unu	14 dek kvar	21 dudek unu	24 dudek kvar	34 tridek kvar
Finnish	—	—	1 yksi	2 kaksi	—	—	9 yhdeksan	7 seitseman	11 yksitoista
French	1 un	6 six	2 deux	3 trois	4 quatre	17 dix-sept	14 quatorze	21 vingt-et-un	23 vingt-trois
Gaelic	—	—	2 a dha	1 a h-aon	8 a h-ochd	7 a seachd	4 a ceithir	11 a h-aon deug	18 a h-ochd deug
German	—	11 elf	1 eins	6 sechs	7 sieben	20 zwanzig	13 dreizehn	—	—
Greek	—	1 ena	3 tria	5 pente	11 enteka	4 tessera	13 dekatria	15 dekapente	23 eikosi tria
Hungarian	5 ot	1 egy	4 negy	2 ketto	9 kilenc	15 tizenot	11 tizenegy	14 tizennegy	12 tizenketto
Irish	—	2 a do	3 a tri	1 a haon	8 a hocht	7 a seacht	15 cuigdeag	4 a ceathair	17 seachtdeag
Italian	—	1 uno	8 otto	7 sette	5 cinque	4 quattro	15 quindici	29 ventinove	19 diciannove
Maltese	—	1000 elf	11 hdax	2 tnejn	1 wiehed	8 tmienja	400 erba' mija	111 mija u hdax	102 mija u tnejn
Norwegian	1 en	3 tre	4 fire	18 atten	11 elleve	13 tretten	24 tjuefire	33 trettitre	34 trettifire
Polish	—	2 dwa	3 trzy	1 jeden	4 cztery	103 sto trzy	9 dziewiec	12 dwanascie	11 jedenascie
Portuguese	1 um	10 dez	2 dois	5 cinco	4 quatro	14 catorze	19 dezanove	16 dezasseis	22 vinte e dois
Romanian	—	1 unu	3 trei	4 patru	—	60 saizeci	20 douazeci	40 patruzeci	11 unsprezece
Russian	—	2 dva	1 odin	6 shest'	4 chetyre	1 000 000 million	20 dvadtsat'	50 pyat'desyat	12 dvenadtsat'
Serbo-Croat	—	2 dva	6 sest	1 jedan	4 cetiri	50 pedeset	12 dvanaest	11 jedanaest	17 sedamnaest
Spanish	—	1 uno	3 tres	5 cinco	4 cuatro	14 catorce	40 cuarenta	16 dieciseis	17 diecisiete
Swedish	1 en	2 tva	4 fyra	20 tjugo	15 femton	13 tretton	22 tjugotva	24 tjugofyra	32 trettiotva
Turkish	3 uc	1 bir	4 dort	8 sekiz	14 on dort	18 on sekiz	21 yirmi bir	24 yirmi dort	28 yirmi sekiz
Welsh	1 un	2 dau	5 pump	7 saith	4 pedwar	11 un deg un	12 un deg dau	15 un deg pump	17 un deg saith

Smallest number containing number of letters

Language	Eleven	Twelve	Thirteen	Fourteen	Fifteen
English	23 twenty-three	73 seventy-three	3000 three thousand	101 a hundred and one	104 a hundred and four
Cornish	80 peswar-ugans	22 dau-warn-ugans	21 onen-warn-ugans	26 whegh-warn-ugans	24 peswar-warn-ugans
Czech	21 dvacet jedna	46 ctyricet sest	41 ctyricet jedna	71 sedmdesat jedna	146 sto ctyricet sest
Danish	31 enogtredive	33 treogtredive	34 fireogtredive	53 treoghalvtreds	54 fireoghalvtreds
Dutch	31 eenendertig	21 eenentwintig	22 tweeentwintig	27 zeven en twintig	77 zeven en zeventig
Esperanto	44 kvardek kvar	121 cent dudek unu	124 cent dudek kvar	134 cent tridek kvar	144 cent kvardek kvar
Finnish	12 kaksitoista	109 sata yhdeksan	20 kaksikymmenta	19 yhdeksantoista	17 seitsemantoista
French	24 vingt-quatre	42 quarante-deux	43 quarante-trois	44 quarante-quatre	54 cinquante-quatre
Gaelic	17 a seachd deug	14 a ceithir deug	104 ceud's a ceithir	80 ceithir fichead	22 a dha air fhichead
German	101 hunderteins	106 hundertsechs	21 einundzwanzig	22 zweiundzwanzig	26 sechsundzwanzig
Greek	14 dekatessera	35 trianta pente	24 eikosi tessera	34 trianta tessera	94 enenenta tessera
Hungarian	19 tizenkilenc	29 huszonkilenc	39 harminckilenc	89 nyolcvankilenc	99 kilencvenkilenc
Irish	25 cuig is fiche	14 ceathairdeag	27 seacht is fiche	31 aondeag is fiche	24 ceathair is fiche
Italian	14 quattordici	24 ventiquattro	34 trentaquattro	45 quarantacinque	44 quarantaquattro
Maltese	101 mija u wiehed	32 tnejn u tletin	22 tnejn u ghoxrin	21 wiehed u ghoxrin	28 tmienja u ghoxrin
Norwegian	103 hundre og tre	104 hundre og fire	118 hundre og atten	111 hundre og elleve	113 hundre og tretten
Polish	14 czternascie	17 siedemnascie	80 osiemdziesiat	19 dziewietnascie	23 dwadziescia trzy
Portuguese	25 vinte e cinco	24 vinte e quatro	34 trinta e quatro	45 quarenta e cinco	44 quarenta e quatro
Romanian	12 doisprezece	13 treisprezece	17 saptesprezece	23 douazeci si trei	24 douazeci si patru
Russian	11 odinnadtsat'	14 chetyrnadtsat'	26 dvadtsat'shest'	24 dvadtsat'chetyre	54 pyat'desyatchetyre
Serbo-Croat	22 dvadeset dva	26 dvadeset sest	21 dvadeset jedan	24 dvadeset cetiri	44 cetrdeset cetiri
Spanish	25 veinticinco	24 veinticuatro	35 treinta y cinco	34 treinta y cuatro	44 cuarenta y cuatro
Swedish	34 trettiofyra	115 hundrafemton	113 hundratretton	122 hundratjugotva	124 hundratjugofyra
Turkish	68 altmis sekiz	124 yuz yirmi dort	128 yuz yirmi sekiz	168 yuz altmis sekiz	224 iki yuz yirmi dort
Welsh	14 un deg pedwar	27 dau ddeg saith	24 dau ddeg pedwar	47 pedwar deg saith	44 pedwar deg pedwar

| | Smallest number containing number of letters | | | | |
Language	Sixteen	Seventeen	Eighteen	Nineteen	Twenty
English	111	115	113	117	124
Cornish	32	72	34	74	92
Czech	141	171	246	241	271
Danish	74	123	124	131	133
Dutch	117	212	131	121	122
Esperanto	234	244	344	444	1244
Finnish	90	21	22	117	91
French	74	84	97	154	174
Gaelic	21	28	27	24	31
German	27	37	220	213	121
Greek	74	135	124	134	194
Hungarian	129	139	189	199	219
Irish	47	37	44	34	57
Italian	54	124	134	145	144
Maltese	301	132	122	121	128
Norwegian	124	133	134	233	234
Polish	21	24	44	29	49
Portuguese	54	125	124	134	145
Romanian	44	113	117	123	124
Russian	126	124	154	226	224
Serbocroat	74	124	144	174	221
Spanish	54	125	124	135	134
Swedish	132	134	224	232	234
Turkish	228	268	468	868	1268
Welsh	127	124	147	144	224

61   Disturbed years

The problem of the Marangan civil wars (puzzle no. 61) involves an interesting combination of working out allowable patterns, and then solving simultaneous equations to find out the lengths of the reigns. The problem can obviously be generalized to any number of royal houses and any number of periods of rule between them. Each such combination would give rise to equations relating the lengths of the reigns, the time displacements of the houses, and the total time of the civil wars.

As stated in the solution, for the problem as posed there are eight combinations of patterns. These arise from five basic arrangements of the houses. If the houses are labelled A, B, C, then the five arrangements are:

(1) ABABC; (2) ABACB; (3) ABCAB; (4) ABCAC; (5) ABCBC.

(A sixth pattern, ABACA, could only appear if the house of A had zero time displacement.)

The eight combinations of the five arrangements (with relabelling of the houses where appropriate) are shown below.

1. ABABC (1)	2. ABABC (1)	3. ABABC (1)	4. ABACB (2)
BACBA (3)	BCABA (4)	CBABA (5)	BABCA (2)
5. ABACB (2)	6. ABACB (2)	7. ABCAB (3)	8. ABCAC (4)
BCABA (4)	CBABA (5)	CBABA (5)	CBACA (4)

Of these combinations, 1, 4, 7 and 8 separate into two periods, one of two reigns and the other of three. The equations for these can be derived by considering these reduced periods in isolation. For instance, combination 1 can be separated into AB becoming BA, and ABC becoming CBA. There is no overlap of years because each part's reigns are rearranged separately. This suggests a problem: is there a maximum number m of reigns, such that, with n different houses and more than m reigns, all possible combinations are separable?

The other four of the combinations listed above – 2, 3, 5 and 6 – are not separable in this way. However, the equations for each of these force at least one pair of reigns to be the same length. This happens whatever numbers we might specify for time displacements or total duration of the civil wars. This suggests another problem: is there a number of houses and a number of reigns, such that at least one of the possible combinations is not separable and has all lengths of reigns different?

Another line of investigation is to look at what mathematicians would call the 'orbits' of the years under the permutations defined by the dating systems in Maranga and outside. As an example, 1703 in their system is 1805 in ours; 1805 in theirs is 1796 in ours; 1796 then goes to 1787, which goes to 1727, and so on, eventually reaching 1763 as the twenty-fourth number, which goes back to 1703. Trying other starting dates, we see there are four orbits of length 24 and one of length 47. The number and sizes of the orbits aren't though determined by the 'combination' alone (which is no. 3 as listed above); they depend on the displacements and total duration also. Different small solutions using combination 3 give orbits specified by (1 3 5)(7 9 11)(2 4 6 8 10 12) or (1 4 7 10 3)(2 5 8 6 9) or (1 4 2 5 8 6 9 7 10 3).

82   A course in bricklaying

Puzzle no. 82 was about building a wall with a given collection of bricks. As it was posed, there was an irregular assortment of bricks, so there was no obvious pattern to use to find the best arrangement. In trying different arrangements, you probably found a score that was achievable in a number of ways, before discovering one that was a bit better. This seems to be the nature of the problem with irregular collections.

It is tempting to hope that for a given collection of bricks there might be a formula for the maximum theoretical score (for shortest crack), but this is not straightforward. A candidate might be half the average brick size, times one less than the number of courses. Assuming that in going from one course to another you achieve on average the overall half-brick-length average, this is what you would obtain. However, this does not always work, as the illustrated example shows.

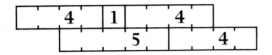

The shortest crack length is 2, but the formula gives $(1/2) \times (18/5) \times 1 < 2$. This is, though, close to the actual answer. For puzzle no. 82 as posed, it gives $(1/2) \times (200/29) \times 9 = 31 + 1/29$, and the highest score known is 31.

In bricklaying practice, the design of 'bonds' (as the patterns are called) does not rely on consideration of minimum crack lengths. For one thing, there is the effect of the strength across the third dimension of the wall. The simplification does, however, produce some relevant patterns.

If the problem is restricted to bricks of only a few different sizes, particular patterns emerge, especially if some sort of regularity is demanded. With just two lengths, a and b, which are forced to alternate along each course, there are two ways in which adjacent rows can overlap, as shown.

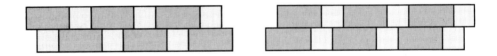

The most regular ways of building these up are also shown.

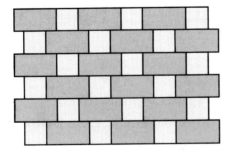 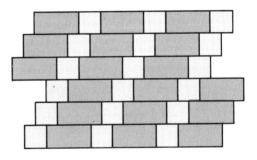

The one on the left is named the Flemish Bond in bricklaying, but there does not seem to be a specific name for the other one.

The Flemish Bond has a crack length of $(a-b)/2$ per course, and the other a length of $b/2$ (in both cases assuming $a > b$). The Flemish is therefore better if $a > 2b$, and the other if $a < 2b$. For a standard building brick $a = 2b$, and the two provide the same crack length.

If the alternation of the two sizes along each course is dropped, but equal numbers of the two sorts are still to be used, then another sort of pattern emerges as best. This is to have several courses entirely of long bricks ('stretchers'), then several entirely of short bricks ('headers'). If a repeated vertical pattern is demanded, then designs like the one shown are obtained.

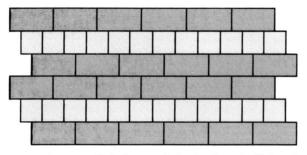

This is called the English Garden Wall Bond.

By imposing some extra rules like these, various patterns may be found. If, for instance, we have three bricks of sizes $a \geqslant b \geqslant c$ (without loss of generality), which must repeat in that order along each course, with each course displaced relative to the previous one by the same amount, then there are five basically different patterns. Four of these are the best choices in different conditions, and these are shown in the diagrams here and on the next page.

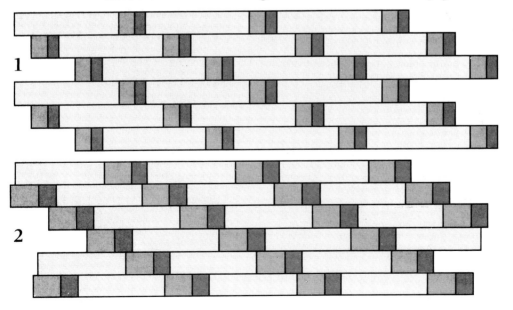

For simplicity, write $T = a + b + c$.

Then if $a > \frac{3}{4}T$, pattern 1 is best, using a course-to-course displacement of anything between $b + c$ and a, and giving an average crack length per course of $(2a - T)/2$.

If $\frac{7}{12}T < a < \frac{3}{4}T$ and $b < \frac{1}{4}T$, then pattern 2 is best, with a displacement of $(5T - 4a)/8$, giving an average length of $(4a - T)/8$.

If $b > \frac{1}{4}T$ and $c < \frac{1}{6}T$, pattern 3 is best, with a displacement of $(T - 2c)/4$ and a length of $(T - 2c)/4$.

If $a < \frac{7}{12}T$ and $c > \frac{1}{6}T$, pattern 4 is best, with a displacement of $\frac{1}{6}T$ and a length of $\frac{1}{6}T$.

If instead we demand that the order of the bricks reverses with each course $(a,b,c,a,b,c, \ldots$ then $a,c,b,a,c,b, \ldots,$ etc.), then there are a further five basically different patterns, but one particular one is always the best; this is shown in the diagram.

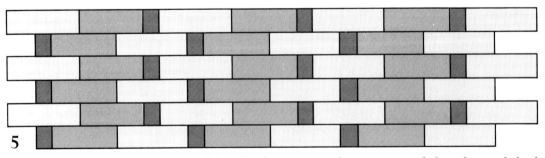

This pattern 5 has displacement and average crack length equal, both being the smaller of $b/2$ and $(a - c)/2$.

If we may choose from either the order remaining the same or reversing each course, then only two of the patterns are in contention.

If $a < \frac{1}{2}T$ and $b > \frac{1}{3}T$, or if $a < \frac{1}{2}T$ and $a - c > \frac{1}{3}T$ then pattern 5 is best.

If $a < \frac{1}{2}T$ and $b < \frac{1}{3}T$, or if $a < \frac{1}{2}T$ and $a - c < \frac{1}{3}T$ then pattern 4 is best.

90 Fixtures and fittings

The question on fixtures in the World Cup second round (puzzle no. 90) has other ramifications. As was remarked, the arrangement that FIFA actually use produces the greatest overall leeway for fitting the teams in. (Maybe that is deliberate, to give them greater control, because they don't actually reveal how they make the choice between the two, or possibly four, alternatives.) Over the 15 possible selections of four teams to qualify, there is a total of 32 alternatives. Much better would seem to be the completely symmetrical arrangement of, say, ABC, ADE, BEF, CDF, which gives two alternatives every time, and thus has an overall total of 30 alternatives. This is the second highest overall total possible.

Selections with fewer alternatives are much more irregular. All selections except the two just mentioned have only one alternative for at least some of the cases of four qualifying teams. The lowest overall leeway is 21, given for instance by ABC, ABD, ABE, ABF.

One could go even further with this question – far beyond the World Cup! If we have n teams, r venues, and with m teams to be placed at each venue, then we have to cater for $n - mr$ teams being eliminated. What suitable arrangements are there for $n - mr + m$ teams to be assigned to each venue, so that whichever $n - mr$ teams are eliminated there will always be at least one possible assignment of teams to venues? What leeways could there be, and what are the 'best' arrangements?

99 Winning innings

In the one-day cricket game of puzzle no. 99, the number of balls and the various probabilities were chosen so that a team playing safely throughout could expect to score the same on average as a team playing riskily throughout. The safe team would usually run out of balls, and the risky team would usually run out of wickets, but the expected score for both is 80. With judicious mixing of the two styles, though, one can expect to score noticeably more.

The important point about the scoring probabilities is that playing riskily gives a better chance of scoring a run, and a better chance of getting out, but provides a worse ratio of runs to wickets. If any of these conditions did not hold, then one of the two tactics would dominate throughout. A similar consideration would apply if there were more than two levels of risk: if any pair did not satisfy the conditions, then one of the pair of tactics could be discounted in favour of the other.

The tactics for batting first that were stated in the solution were derived as follows. Suppose that from a given point we had to commit ourselves to one tactic or the other; which would lead to the greater expected score? By considering whether we run out of balls or wickets first, we can state that:

(a)   playing safely, the expected score is the lower of $0.4b$ and $20w$;
(b)   playing riskily, the expected score is the lower of $0.8b$ and $8w$.

(In this and the following, b will be the number of balls left, w will be the number of wickets left, and r will be the number of runs scored if batting first or the number of runs behind if batting second.)

If $b > 50w$, then both tactics run out of wickets, so playing safely is the better tactic as the expectation is another $20w$ runs.

If $b < 10w$, then both tactics run out of balls, so playing riskily is the better tactic as the expectation is another $0.8b$ runs.

If $50w > b > 10w$, then playing safely gives an expectation of another $0.4b$ runs, and playing riskily gives an expectation of another $8w$ runs. Therefore we should play safely when $0.4b > 8w$.

This last condition also subsumes the two conditions just derived, and it is of course identical to the form $b > 20w$ used in the solution.

Although the above does give a reasonable rough guide, it is not necessarily completely accurate. What really matters is not the expected score, but the probability of winning. There's no credit in an overall scoring system in winning games by large margins; just winning is what's important! The rigorous way to approach the game as described is to compute the recurrence relations for probabilities of winning. To do this, you have to examine the second innings first! Starting with the boundary conditions of no balls left or no wickets left, the probabilities can be found, together with whether it is appropriate to play safely or riskily in any given situation. When this has been completed, and you know the chance of the second team winning when it starts its innings so many runs behind, you can then work backwards through the first team's innings, and work out its probabilities and tactics.

Unfortunately, the problem is not readily soluble by hand or analytically, and on a computer rounding errors eventually build up. Computer calculations of the probabilities did though suggest the rule for batting second that was stated in the solution. The probability of winning when following that rule was in all situations within one part in a million of the calculated 'optimal' probability.

The build-up of rounding errors did though obscure the situation when analysing the first innings. It was, however, clear that there is no simple linear inequality to indicate the correct tactics. Plotting 'critical' numbers of runs (at or above which you should play safe, below which you should play riskily) against the number of balls and wickets left showed a curved surface, not an inclined plane. A rough approximation to the surface is given by the following combination of conditions:

(a)   if $b < 12w - 4$, play safely if

$$(12w - 5)r > -970.9 + 2408.4w - (8.4w + 29.1)b;$$

(b)   if $12w - 4 \leqslant b < 12w + 10$, play safely if

$$14r > 1985.7 + 1138.1w - 111.48w^2 + (9.3w - 101.6)b;$$

(c)   if $12w + 10 \leqslant b < 9.7w + 47.6$, play safely if

$$(37.6 - 2.3w)r > 2990.0 + 329.7w - 12.2w^2 + (0.9w - 38.7)b;$$

(d)   if $b \geqslant 9.7w + 47.6$, play safely if

$$(23.6 + 1.7w)r > 2174.8 + 471.1w + 19.6w^2 - (1.7w + 30.6)b;$$

(e)   otherwise play riskily.

This is a relatively complicated solution for batting first, but it does produce better results than the simple 'play safely if $b > 20w$'. With $10\,000$ matches simulated for the two cases, the simple tactics averaged 104 and the complicated tactics averaged 105. This seems slight, but playing against the stated rule for batting second the simple tactics had a 42% chance of winning and the complicated tactics had a 45% chance.

This 45% chance of the first team winning agrees with the calculated percentage for 'optimal' tactics. (For simplicity, the 1.3% of ties have been split evenly between wins and losses.) Although this game is a greatly simplified version of one-day cricket, it does bear out what is observed in actual matches, that the side batting second has a slight advantage.

For even further investigation, changes of parameters can be made, and slight alterations to the game rules suggest themselves, but it seems complicated enough as it is!

100   Artful dodgem

For those who like programming games on computers, 'dodgem' lends itself very well. The rules and aim are both very straightforward, and there are relatively few choices for moves at each stage. These points mean that there is little complication beyond the programming of looking n moves ahead; and in operation the process will be quite fast. A very simple evaluation of any position is also effective: find the difference between the number of moves that white would take and the number that black would take to get all his or her pieces off the board, if there were no obstructions by opposing pieces. For more adventurous programming, slight changes could be made to this evaluation sum, or the details of looking ahead. But even without these enhancements, a computer program can play a very good game on the 3 × 3 board when looking only a few moves ahead.